HAL•LEONARD®
GUITAR
PLAY-ALONG

AUDIO
ACCESS
INCLUDED

DREAM THE

CW00329702

VOL. 167

PLAYBACK+
Speed • Pitch • Balance • Loop

To access audio visit:
www.halleonard.com/mylibrary
Enter Code
6442-5551-4502-4457

Cover photo: Nidhal Marzouk

All keyboards and drum sequencing by Chris Romero
All guitars, basses and additional percussion by Jordan Baker

ISBN 978-1-4768-8940-5

HAL•LEONARD®
CORPORATION

7777 W. BLUEMOUND RD. P.O. BOX 13819 MILWAUKEE, WI 53213

In Australia Contact:
Hal Leonard Australia Pty. Ltd.
4 Lentara Court
Cheltenham, Victoria, 3192 Australia
Email: ausadmin@halleonard.com.au

Visit Hal Leonard Online at
www.halleonard.com

VOL. 167

DREAM·THEATER

CONTENTS

Page	Title
6	Breaking All Illusions
32	Erotomania
45	Fatal Tragedy
60	Hell's Kitchen
68	In the Presence of Enemies, Pt. 1
83	Metropolis-Part 1 "The Miracle and the Sleeper"
104	On the Backs of Angels
120	Six Degrees of Inner Turbulence: I. Overture
129	Six Degrees of Inner Turbulence: II. About to Crash
142	Under a Glass Moon
5	GUITAR NOTATION LEGEND

GUITAR NOTATION LEGEND

THE MUSICAL STAFF shows pitches and rhythms and is divided by bar lines into measures. Pitches are named after the first seven letters of the alphabet.

TABLATURE graphically represents the guitar fingerboard. Each horizontal line represents a string, and each number represents a fret.

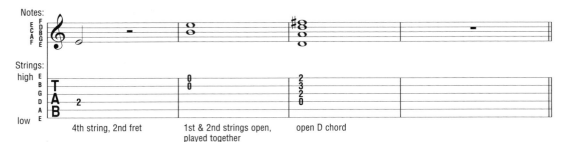

4th string, 2nd fret

1st & 2nd strings open, played together

open D chord

HALF-STEP BEND: Strike the note and bend up 1/2 step.

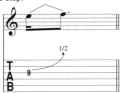

WHOLE-STEP BEND: Strike the note and bend up one step.

GRACE NOTE BEND: Strike the note and immediately bend up as indicated.

SLIGHT (MICROTONE) BEND: Strike the note and bend up 1/4 step.

BEND AND RELEASE: Strike the note and bend up as indicated, then release back to the original note. Only the first note is struck.

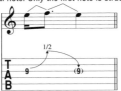

PRE-BEND: Bend the note as indicated, then strike it.

VIBRATO: The string is vibrated by rapidly bending and releasing the note with the fretting hand.

PALM MUTING: The note is partially muted by the pick hand lightly touching the string(s) just before the bridge.

HAMMER-ON: Strike the first (lower) note with one finger, then sound the higher note (on the same string) with another finger by fretting it without picking.

PULL-OFF: Place both fingers on the notes to be sounded. Strike the first note and without picking, pull the finger off to sound the second (lower) note.

LEGATO SLIDE: Strike the first note and then slide the same fret-hand finger up or down to the second note. The second note is not struck.

SHIFT SLIDE: Same as legato slide, except the second note is struck.

TRILL: Very rapidly alternate between the notes indicated by continuously hammering on and pulling off.

TAPPING: Hammer ("tap") the fret indicated with the pick-hand index or middle finger and pull off to the note fretted by the fret hand.

NATURAL HARMONIC: Strike the note while the fret-hand lightly touches the string directly over the fret indicated.

PINCH HARMONIC: The note is fretted normally and a harmonic is produced by adding the edge of the thumb or the tip of the index finger of the pick hand to the normal pick attack.

TREMOLO PICKING: The note is picked as rapidly and continuously as possible.

VIBRATO BAR DIVE AND RETURN: The pitch of the note or chord is dropped a specified number of steps (in rhythm), then returned to the original pitch.

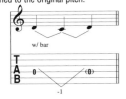

VIBRATO BAR SCOOP: Depress the bar just before striking the note, then quickly release the bar.

VIBRATO BAR DIP: Strike the note and then immediately drop a specified number of steps, then release back to the original pitch.

Additional Musical Definitions

(accent) • Accentuate note (play it louder).

(staccato) • Play the note short.

D.S. al Coda • Go back to the sign (%), then play until the measure marked "*To Coda*," then skip to the section labelled "**Coda**."

D.C. al Fine • Go back to the beginning of the song and play until the measure marked "*Fine*" (end).

Fill • Label used to identify a brief melodic figure which is to be inserted into the arrangement.

N.C. • Harmony is implied.

• Repeat measures between signs.

• When a repeated section has different endings, play the first ending only the first time and the second ending only the second time.

Breaking All Illusions

Music by John Petrucci, John Myung and Jordan Rudess
Lyrics by John Petrucci and John Myung

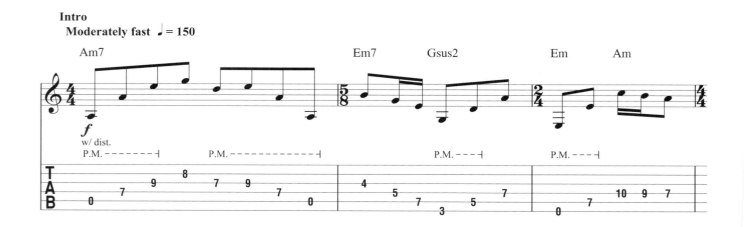

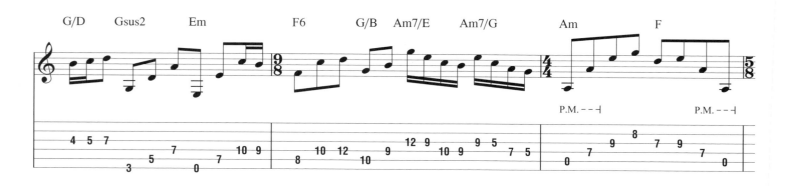

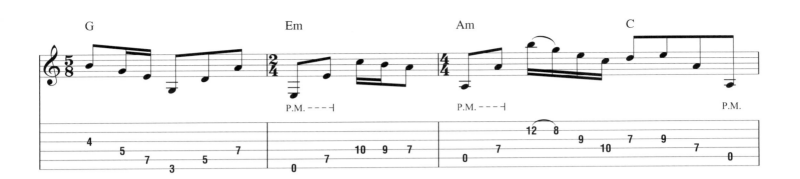

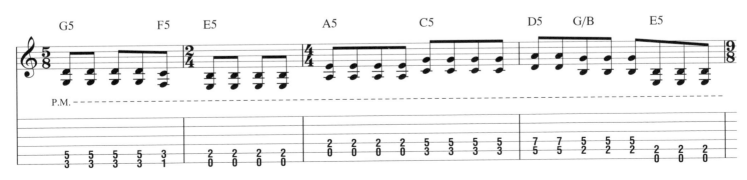

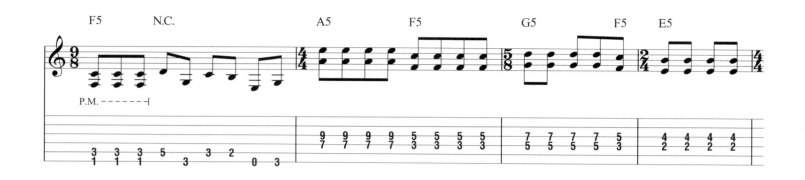

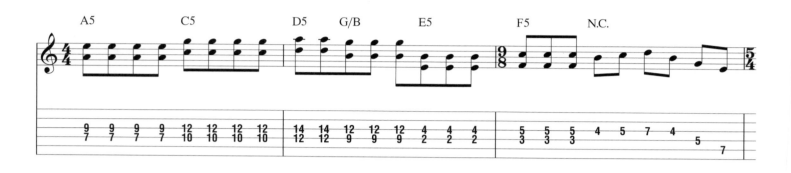

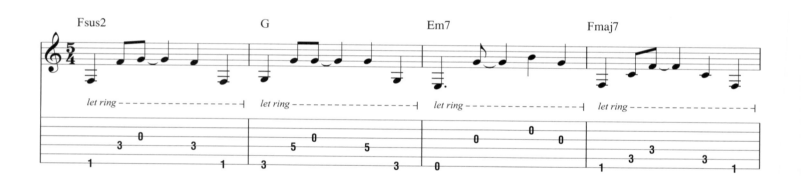

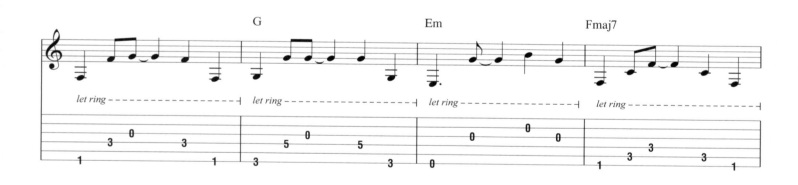

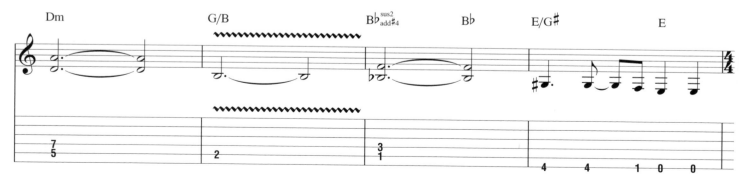

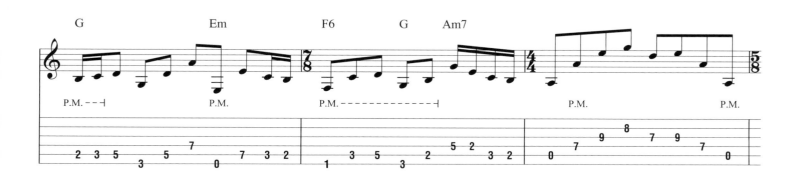

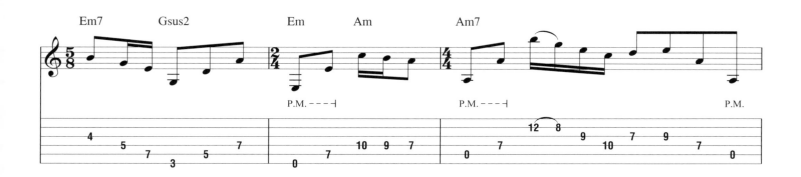

Interlude

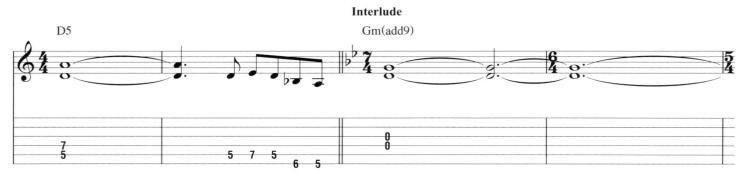

Verse

1. With the sun ___ in place, ___ there's a test ___ of faith. ___ Streams of thought ___ a-
wak - en. ___ New re - al - i - ties, ___ sin - gu - lar - i - ties, ___ ___ break - ing all ___ il - lu - sions. ___

Interlude

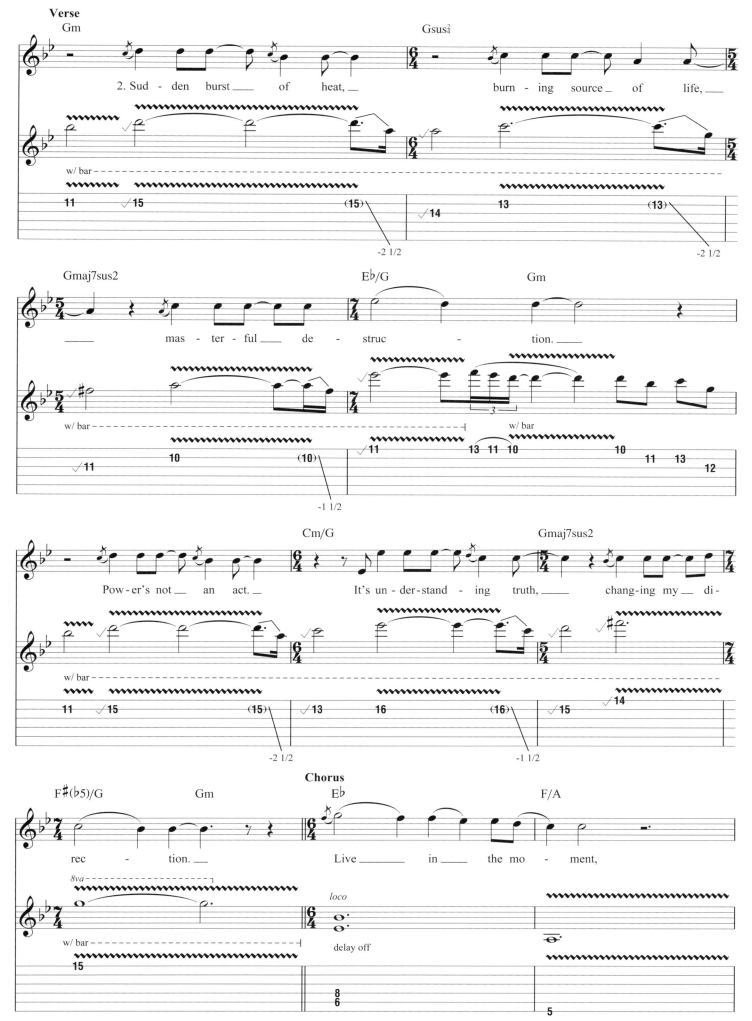

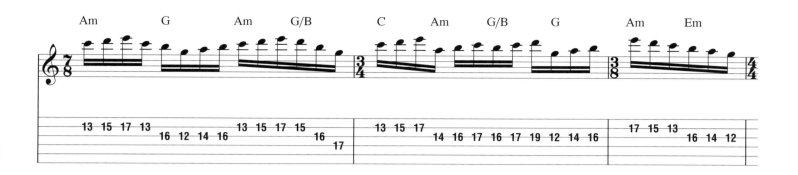

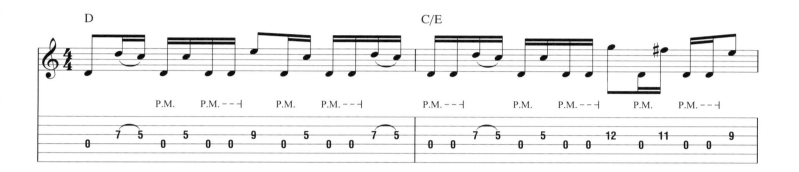

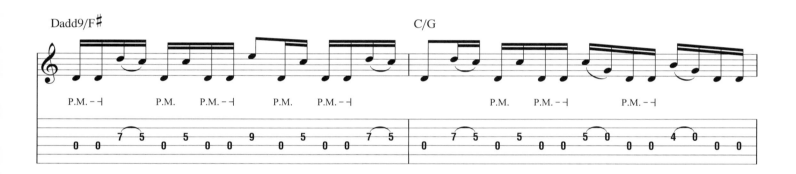

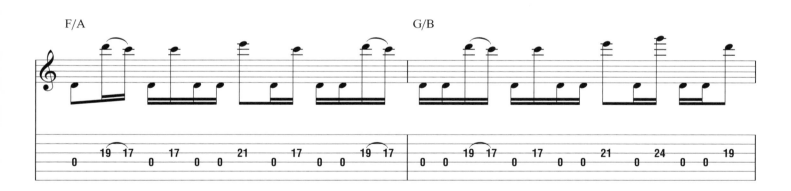

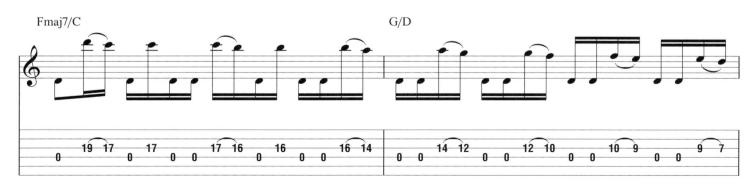

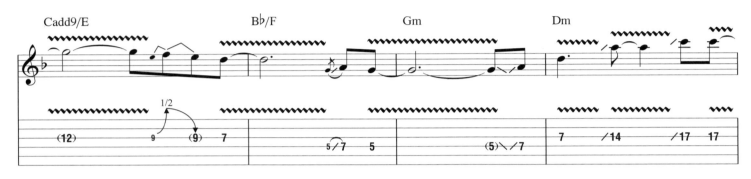

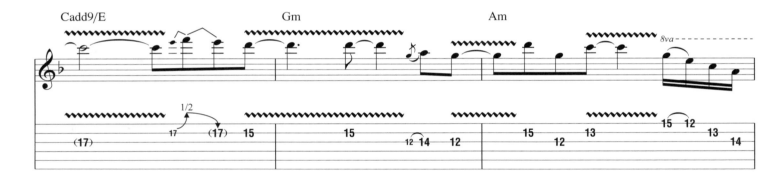

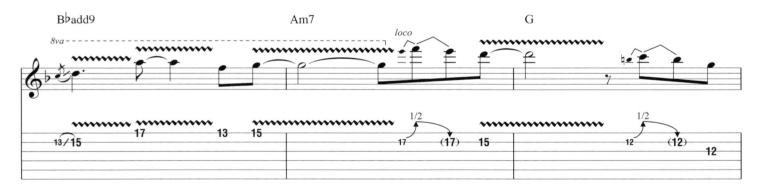

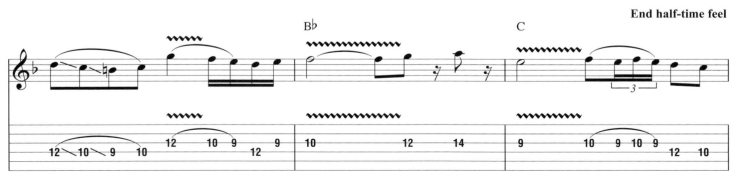

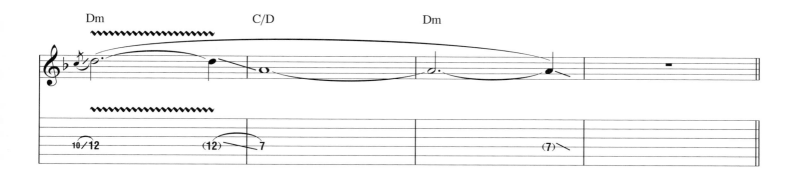

Interlude

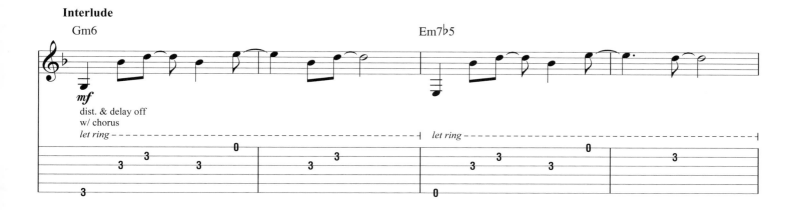

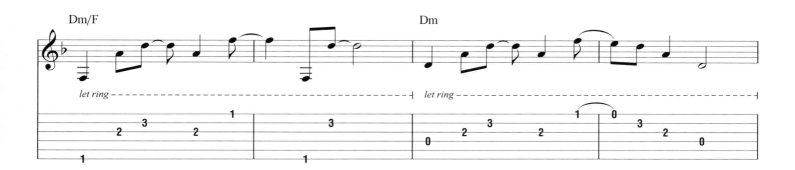

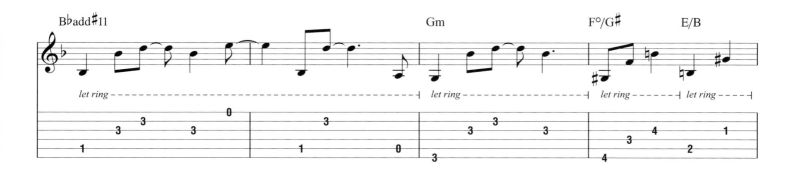

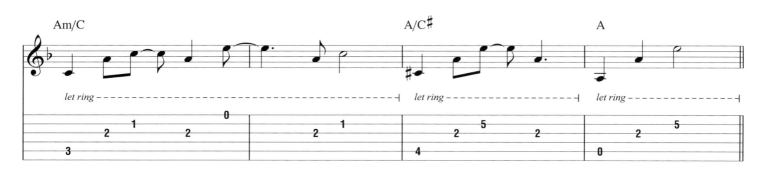

Guitar Solo
Half-time feel

*Played slightly behind the beat.

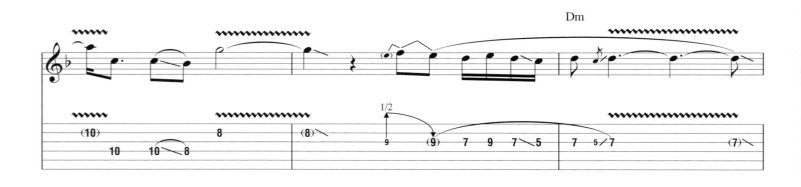

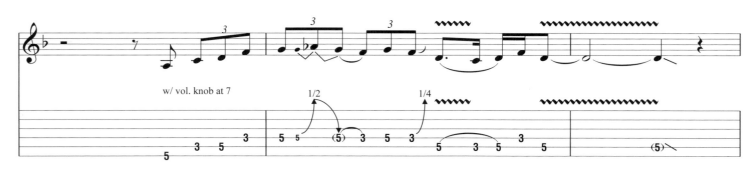

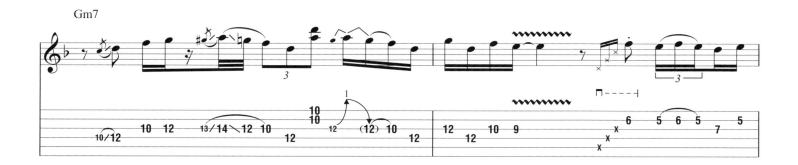

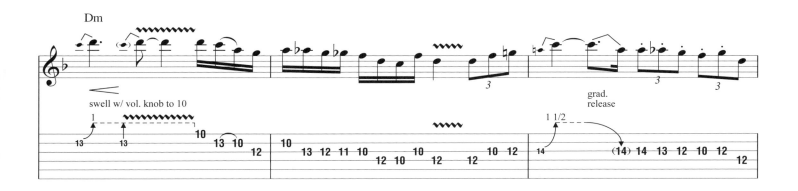

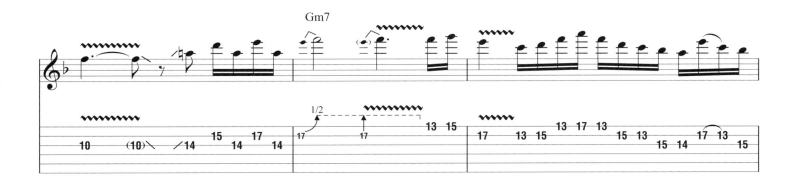

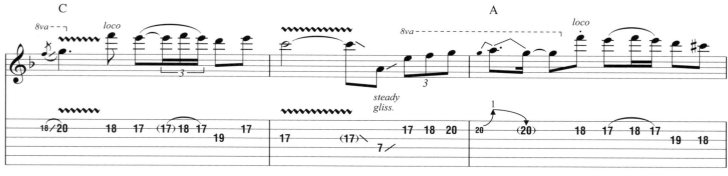
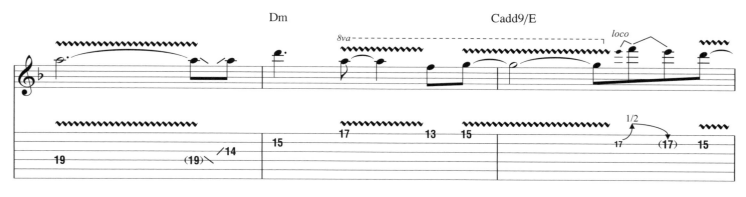

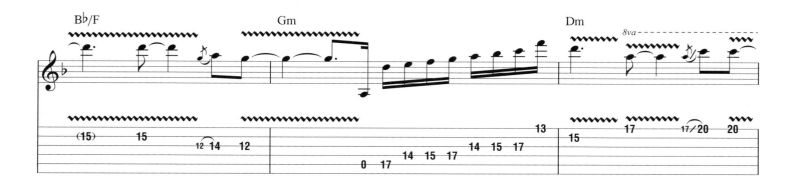

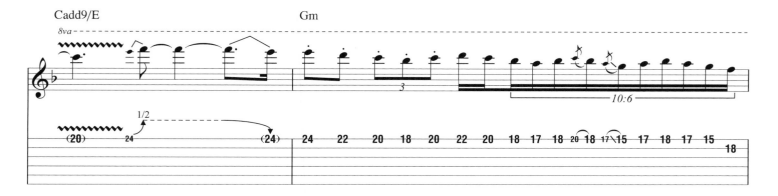

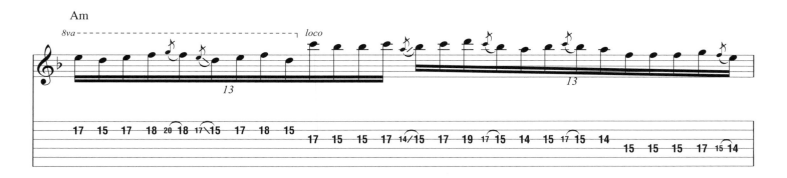

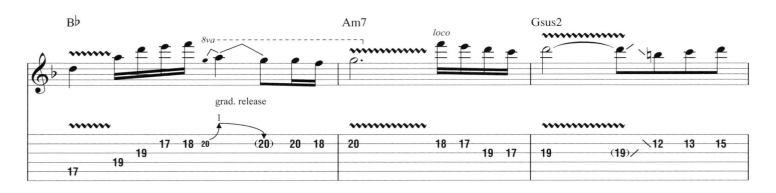

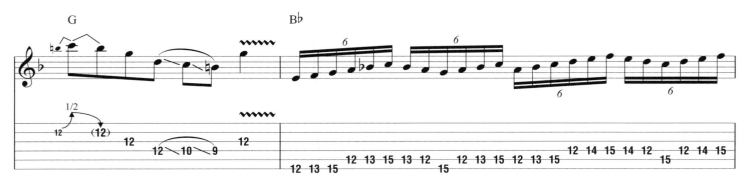

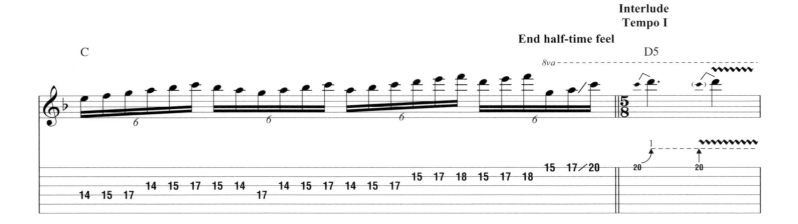

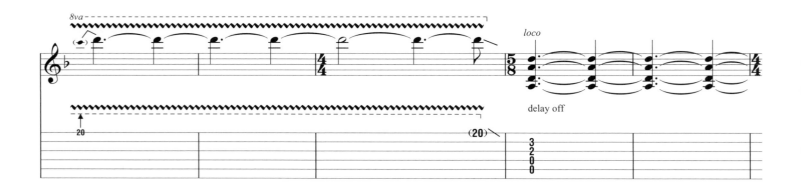

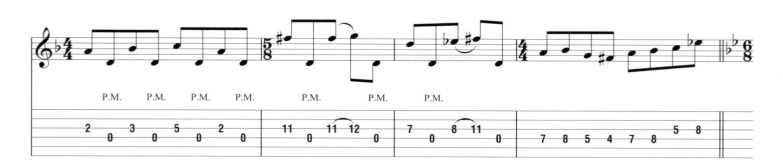

26

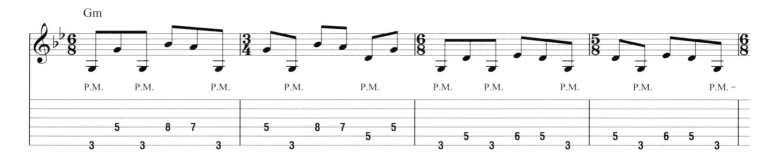

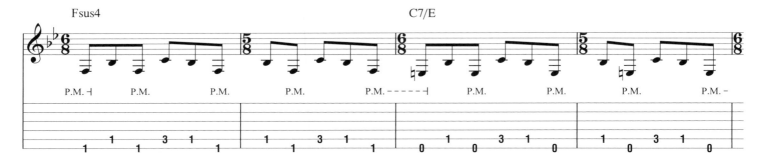

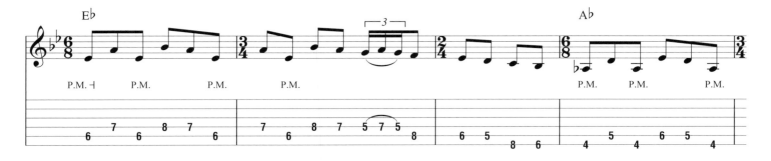

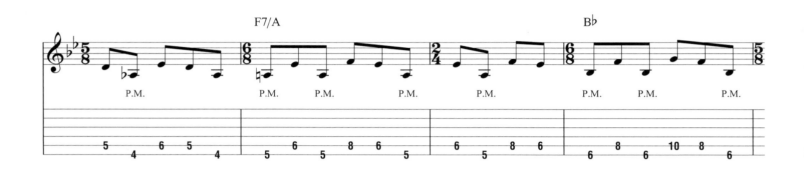

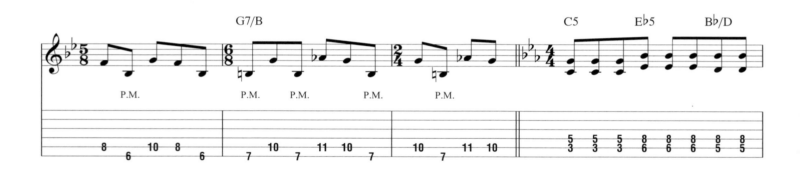

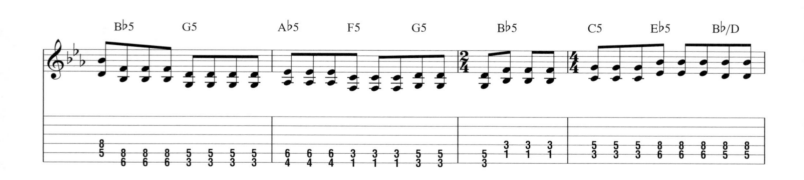

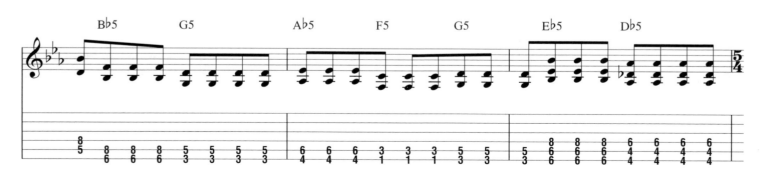

28

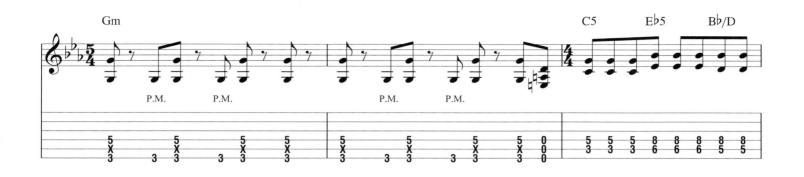

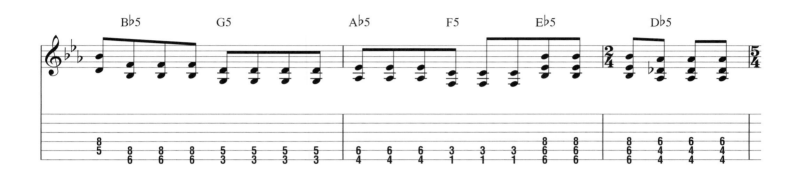

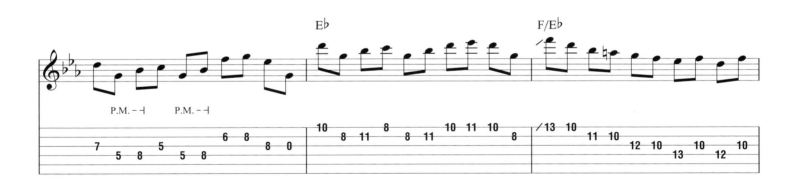

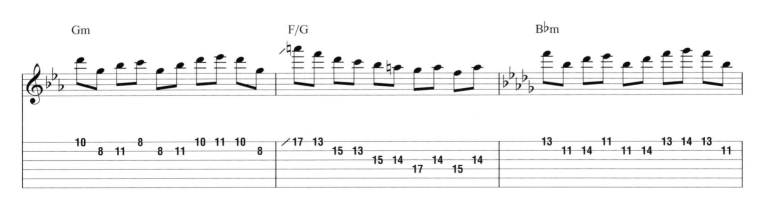

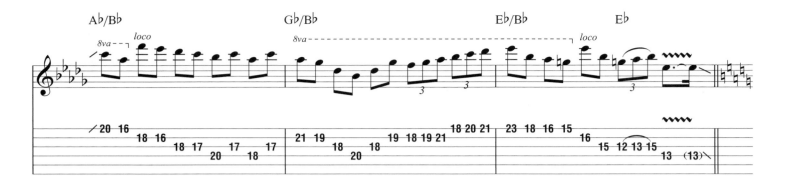

Chorus

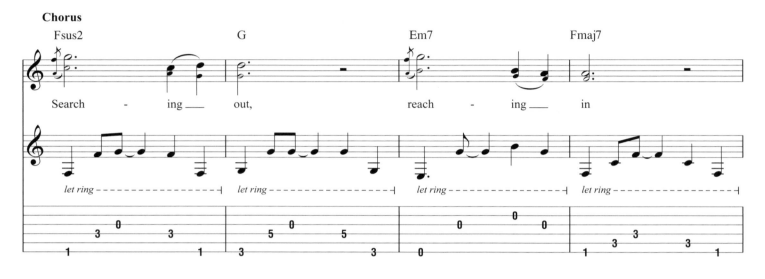

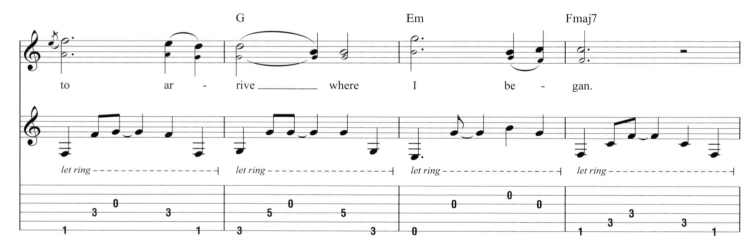

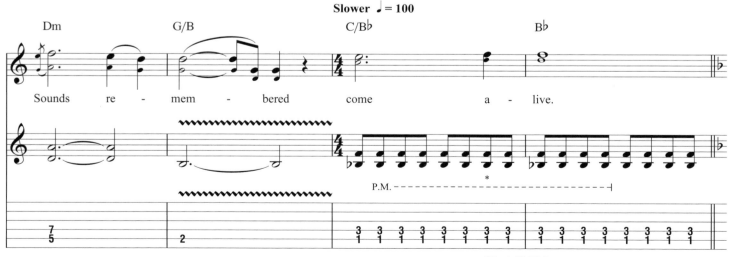

*Grad. lift P.M.

Outro

Erotomania

Music by Kevin LaBrie, Kevin Moore, John Myung, John Petrucci and Michael Portnoy

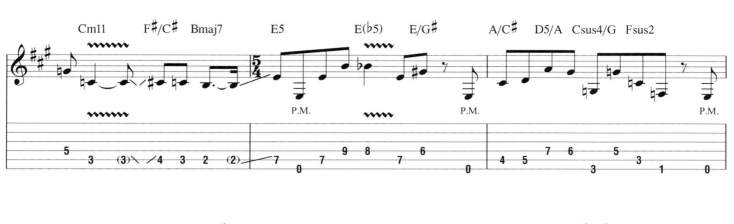

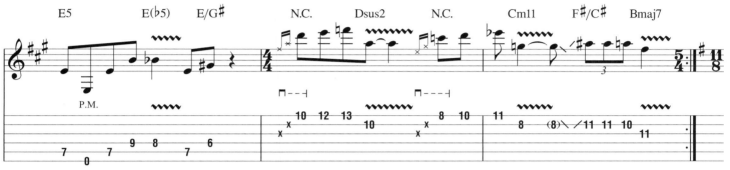

C

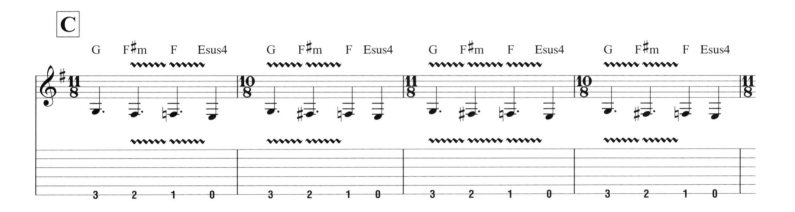

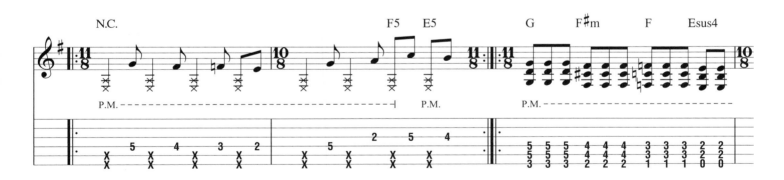

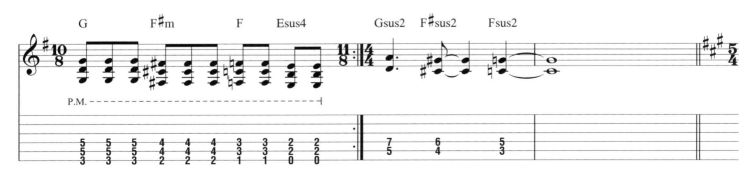

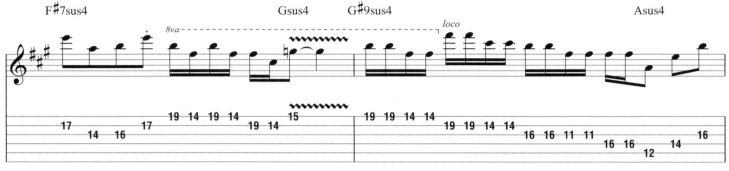

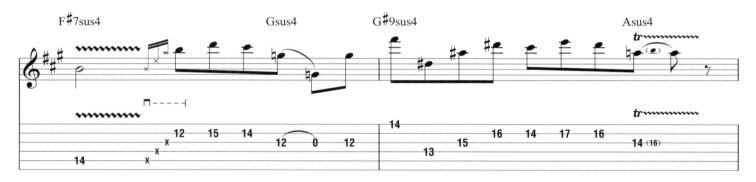

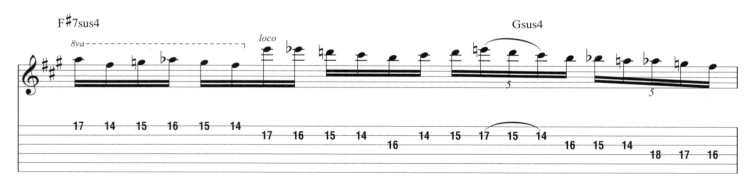

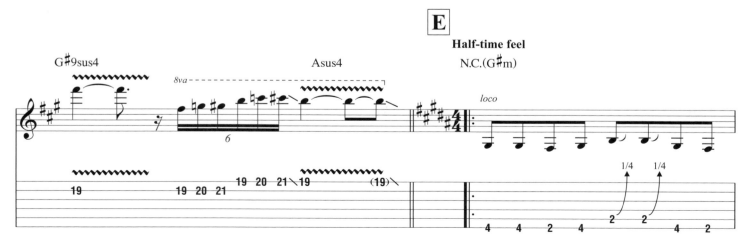

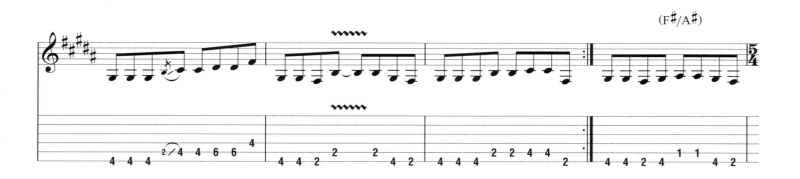

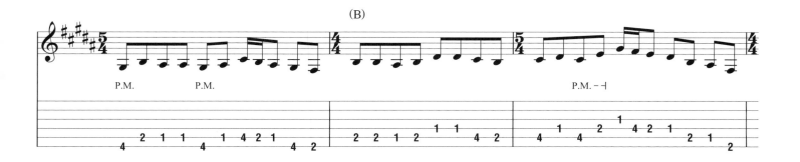

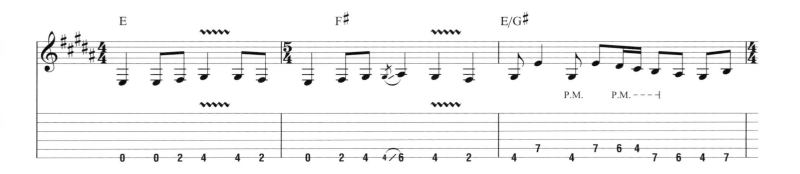

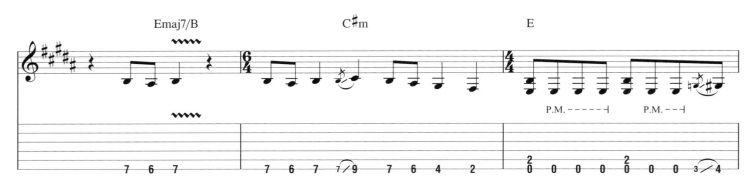

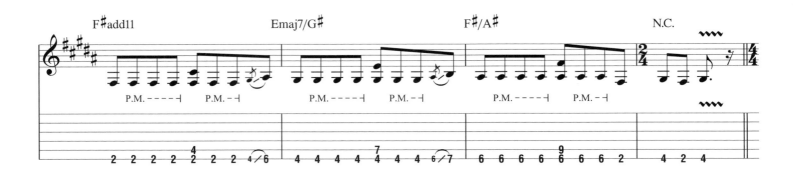

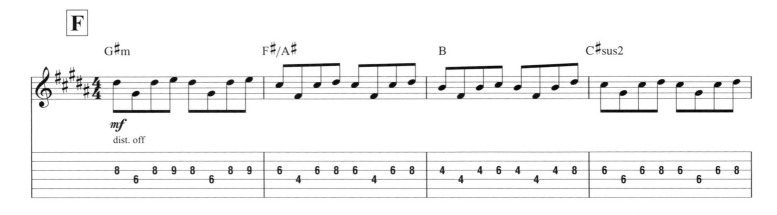

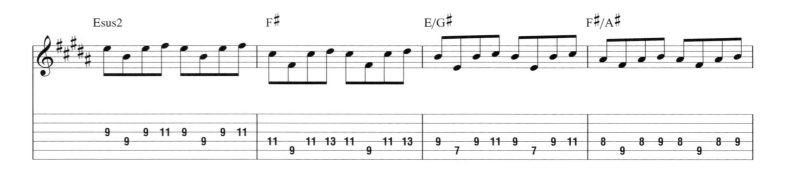

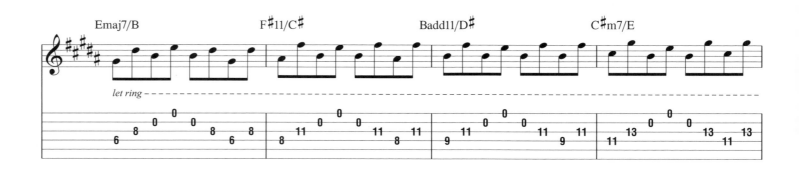

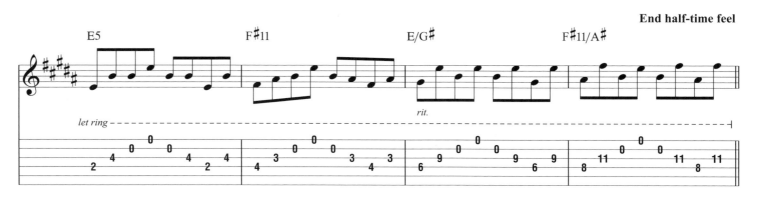

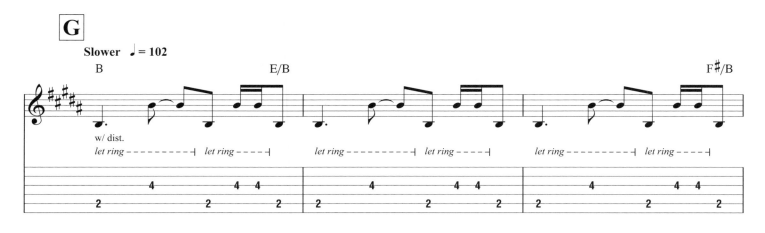

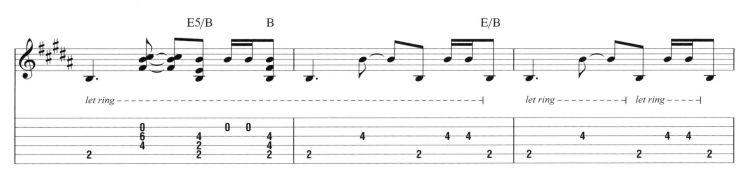

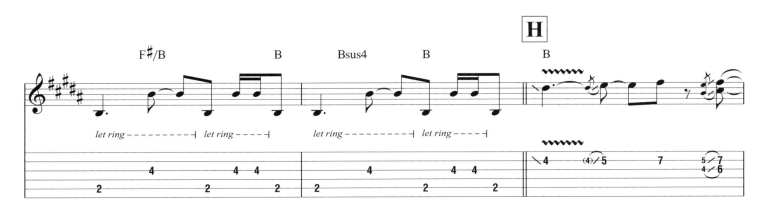

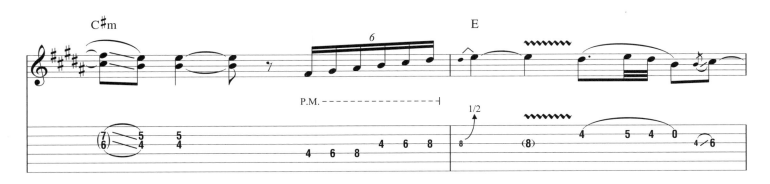

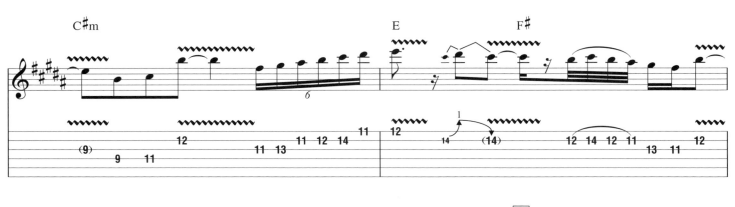

I

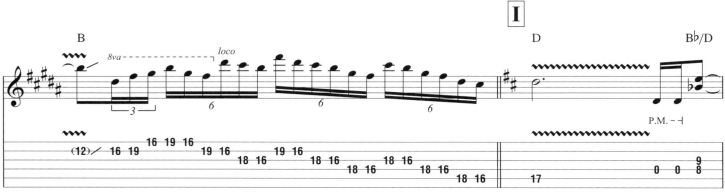

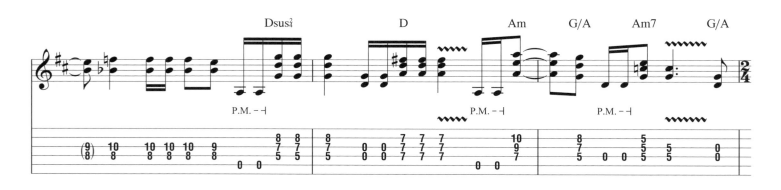

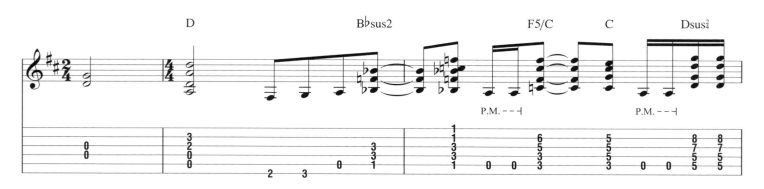

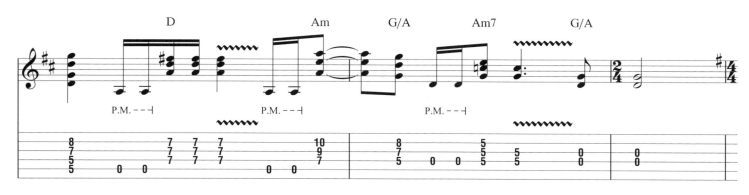

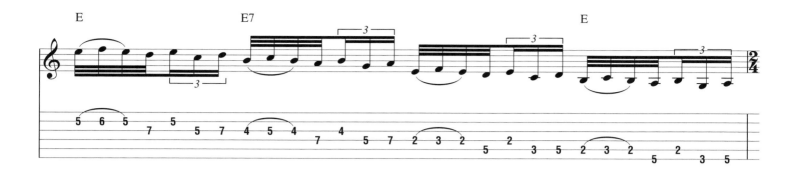

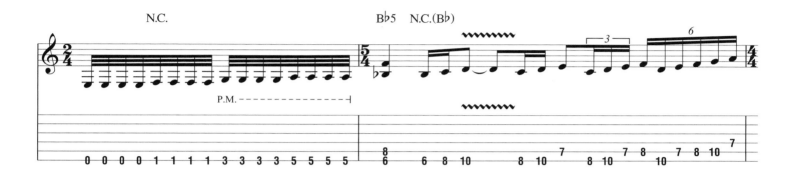

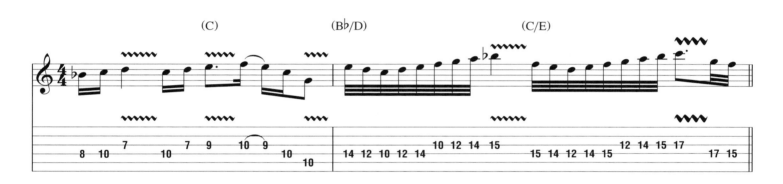

L

Tempo I

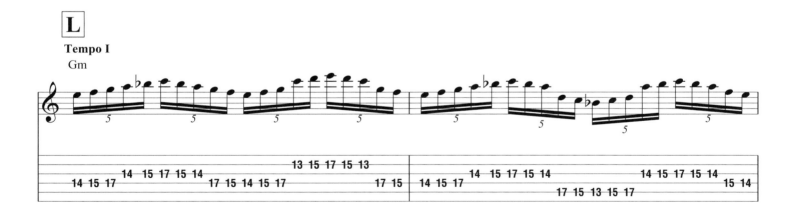

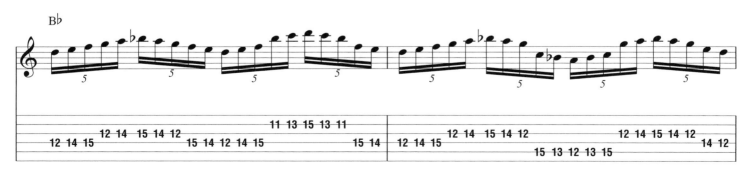

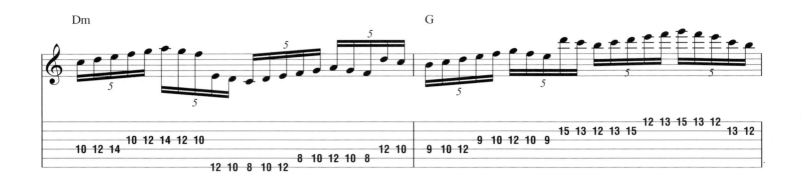

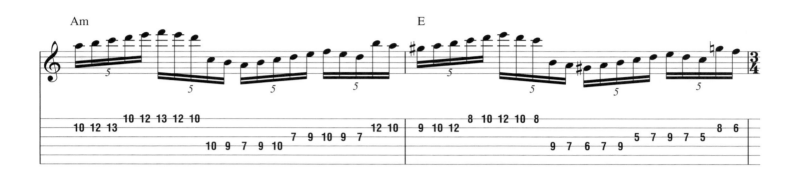

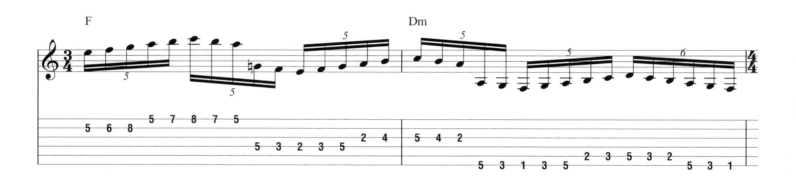

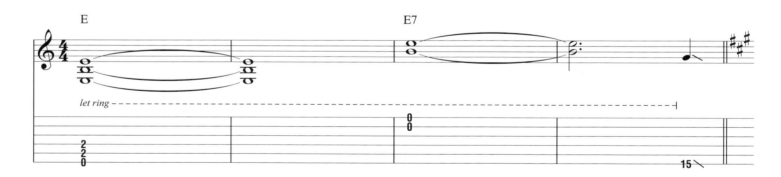

M

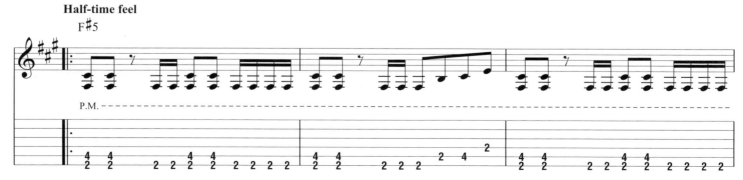

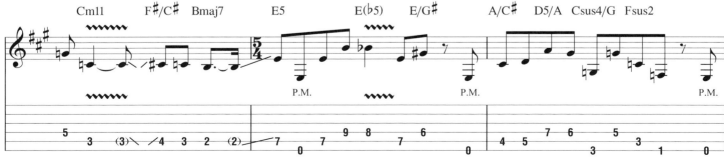

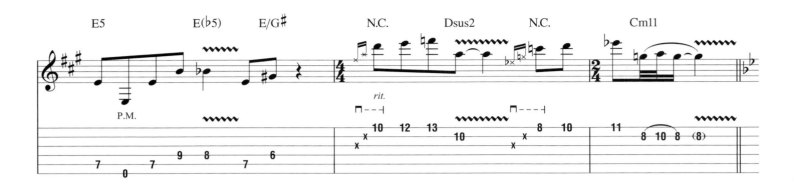

O

Free time
Cm11

*Key signature denotes C Dorian.

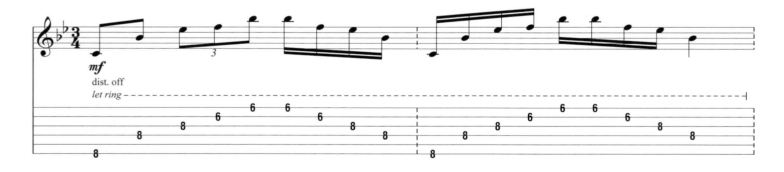

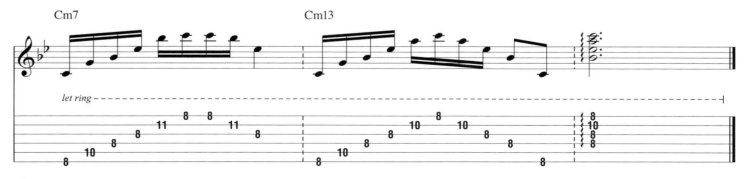

Fatal Tragedy

Words and Music by John Petrucci, Michael Portnoy, John Myung, Jordan Rudess and Kevin LaBrie

Verse

1. I shut the door and trav-eled to an-oth-er home.

I met an old-er man; he seemed to be a-lone. I

felt that I could trust him. He talked to me that night: "Lad,

did you know a girl was mur-dered here? This fa-tal

46

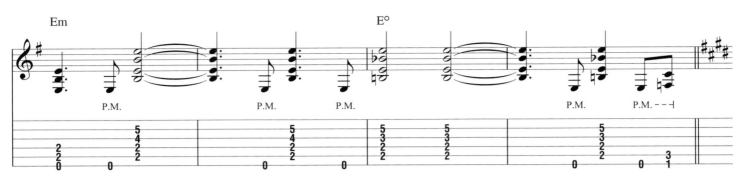

Chorus

With-out __ love, with-out __ truth,... __ (...there can be __ no turn - ing back.) __

End half-time feel

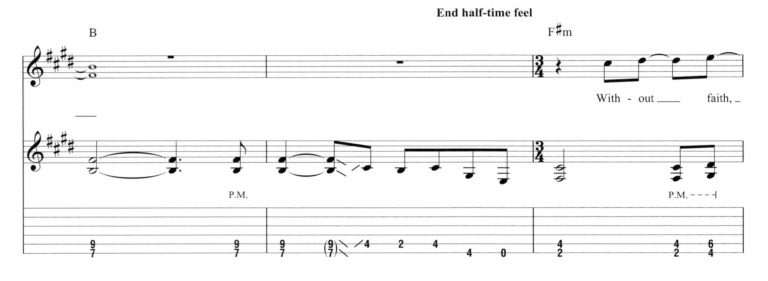

With - out __ faith,

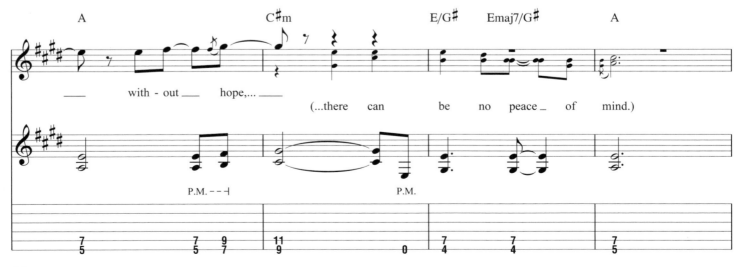

__ with - out __ hope,... __ (...there can be no peace __ of mind.)

50

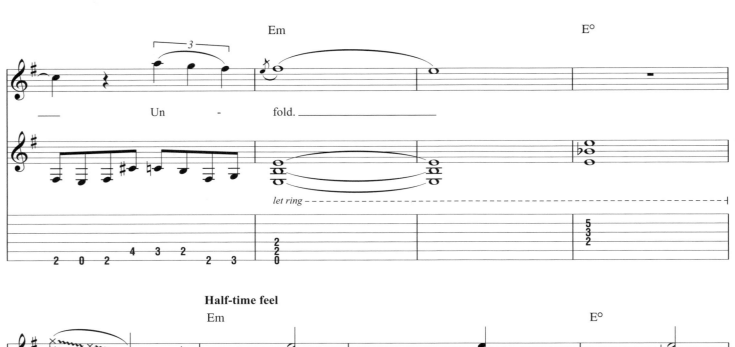

Half-time feel

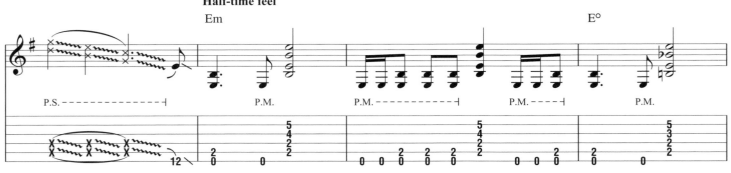

Chorus
End half-time feel

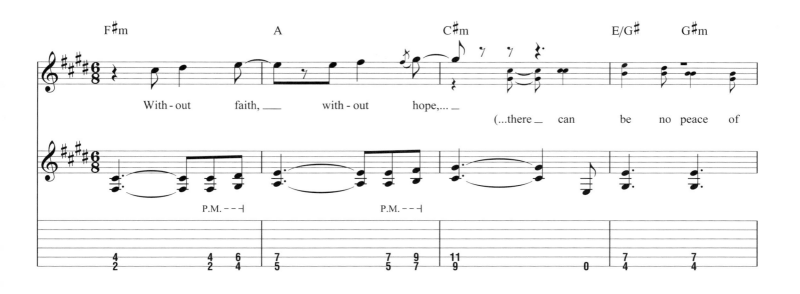

With-out faith, ___ with-out hope,... ___

(...there ___ can be no peace of

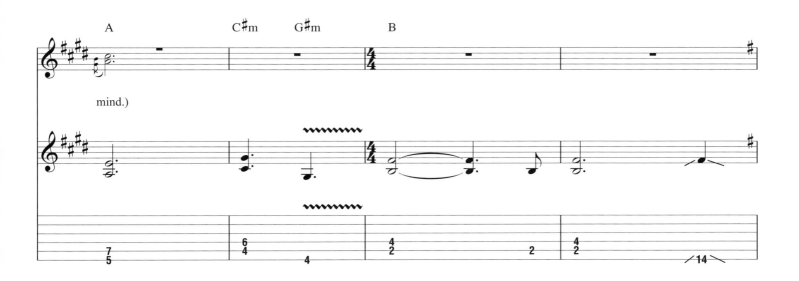

mind.)

Interlude

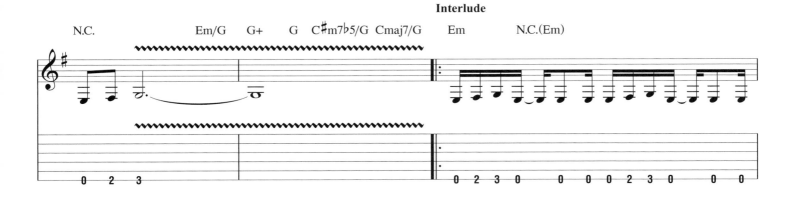

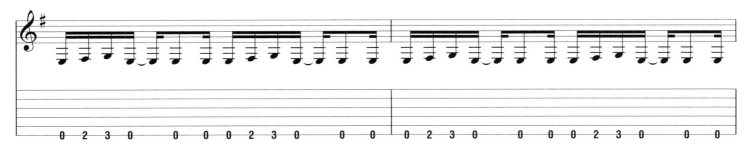

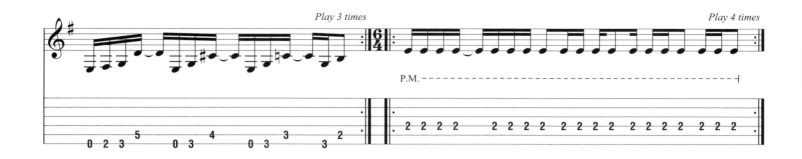

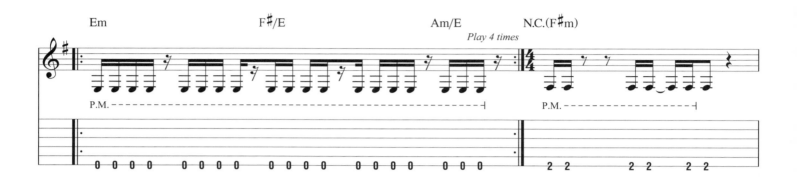

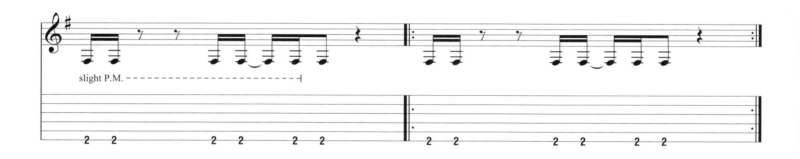

Guitar Solo

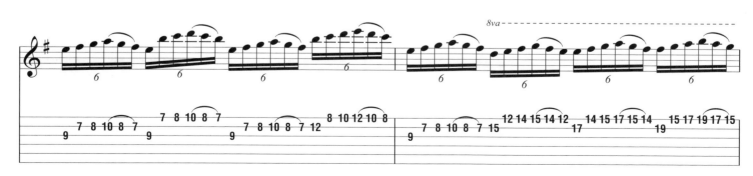

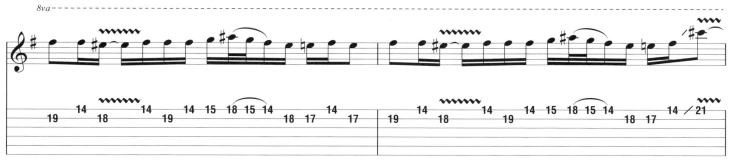

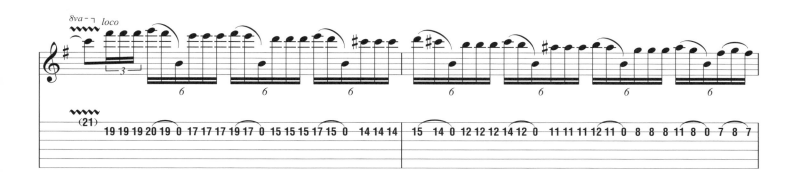

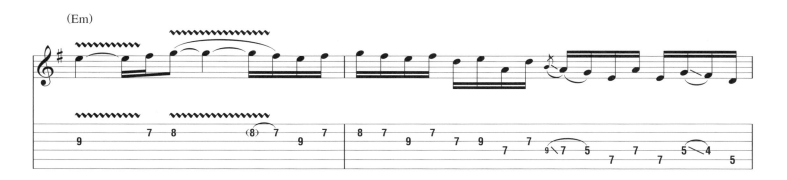

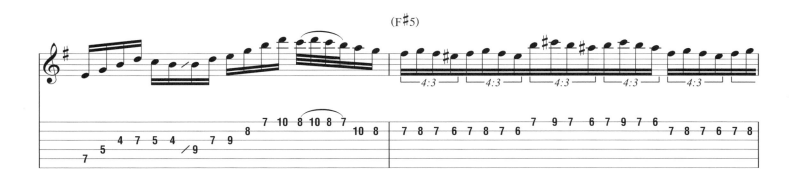

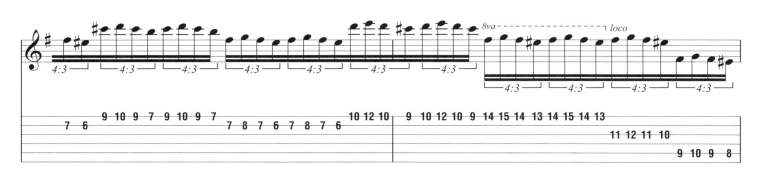

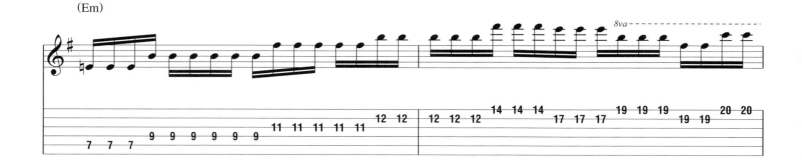

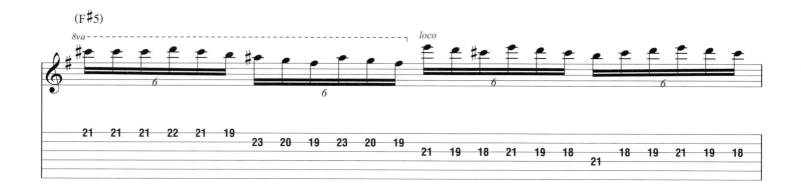

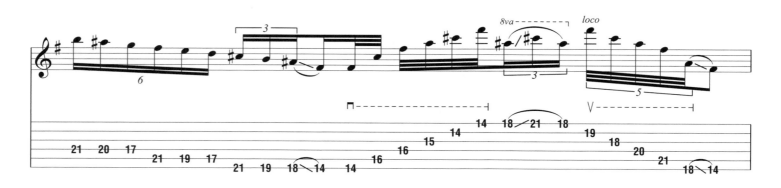

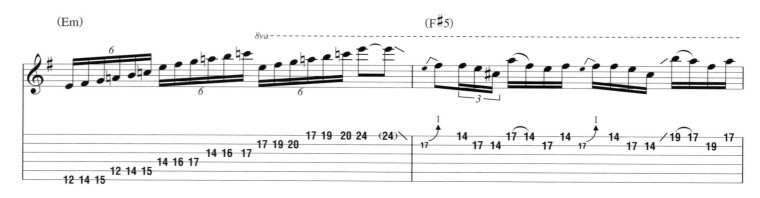

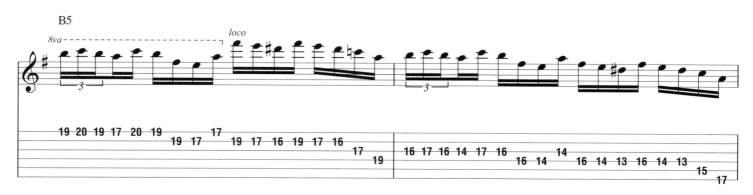

Keyboard Solo

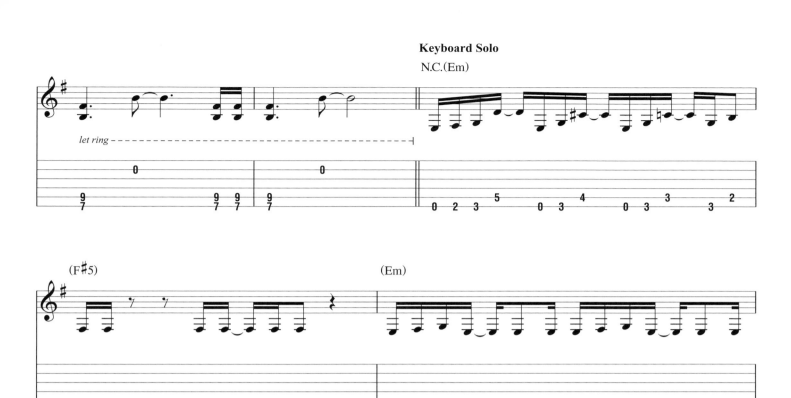

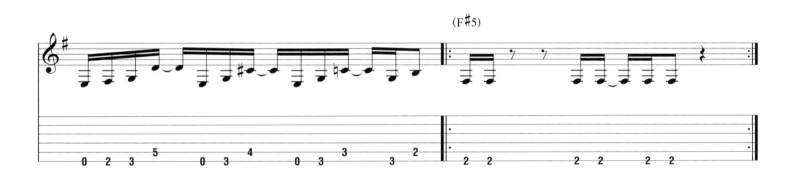

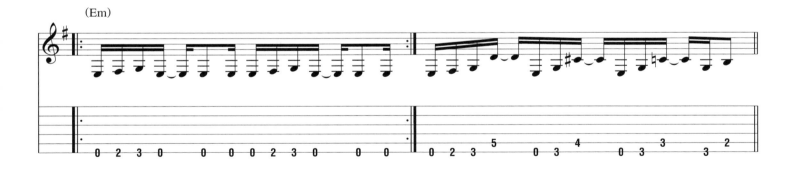

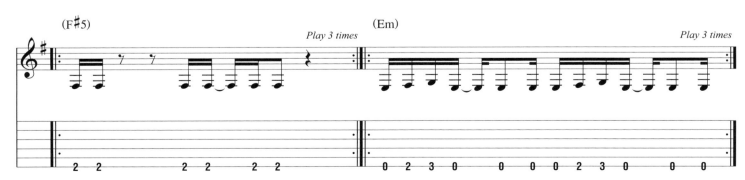

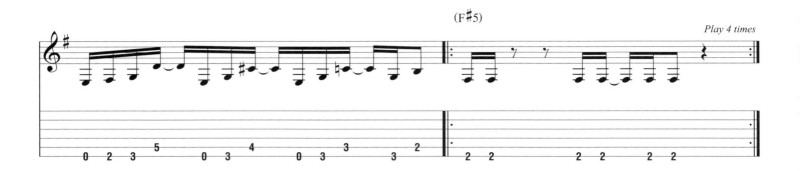

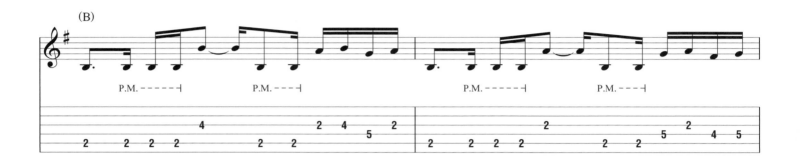

Outro
Double-time feel

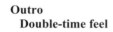

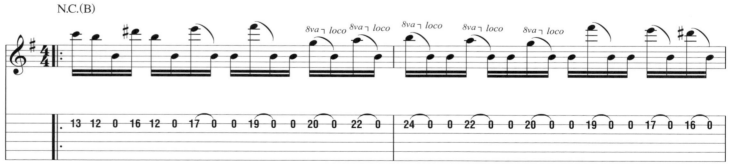

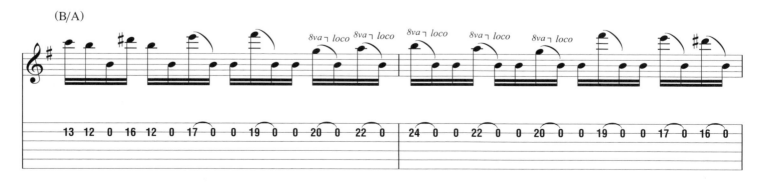

Hell's Kitchen

Words and Music by Michael Portnoy, John Myung, Derek Sherinian and John Petrucci

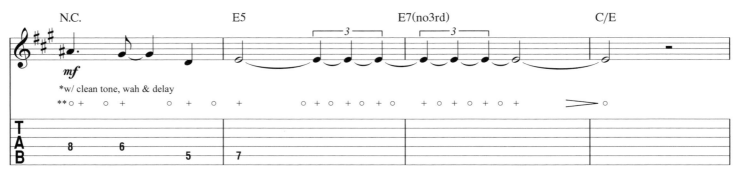

*Delay set for 500 ms regeneration w/ 1 repeat.
**Wah notation: ○ = bass (toe up); + = treble (toe down)

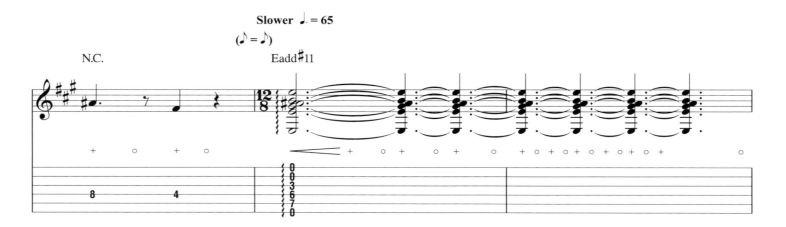

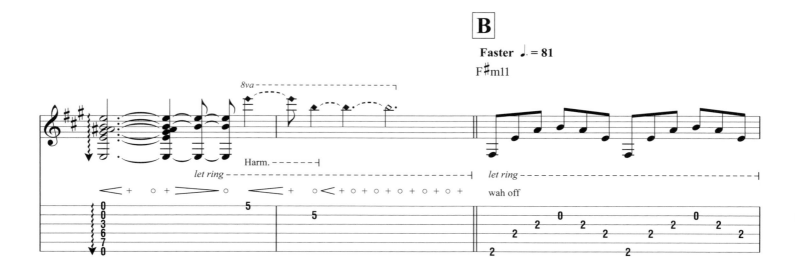

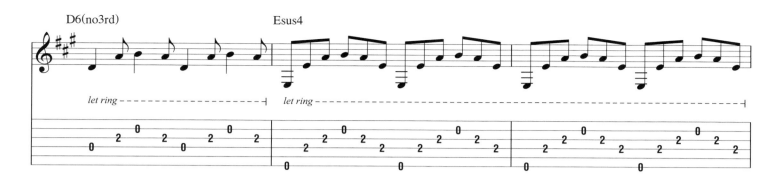

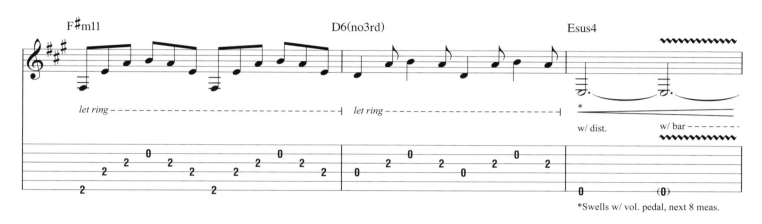

*Swells w/ vol. pedal, next 8 meas.

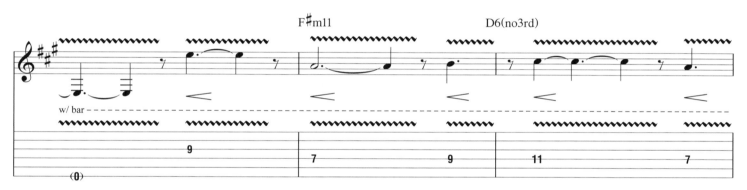

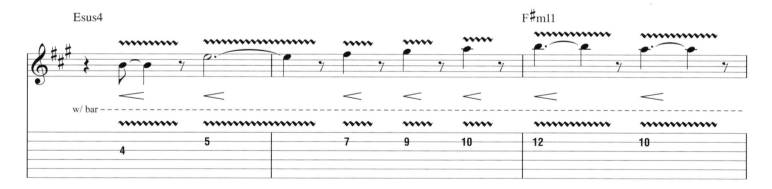

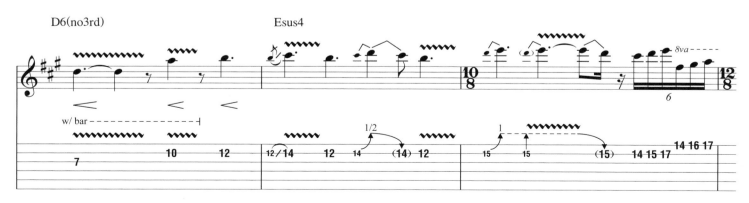

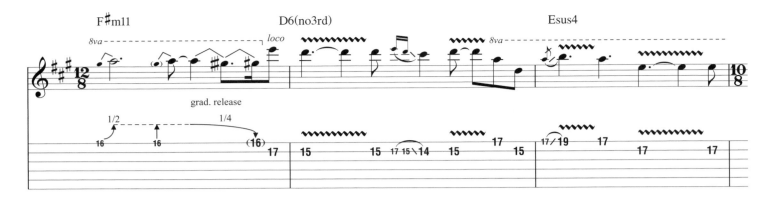

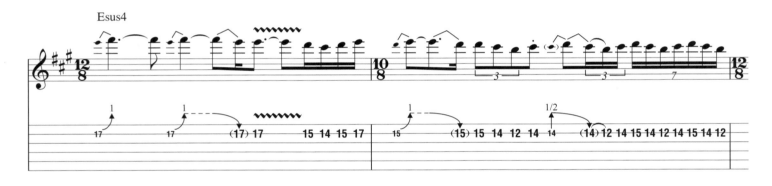

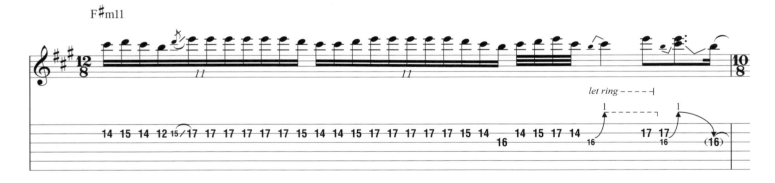

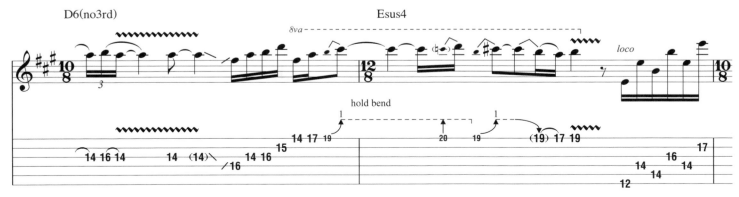

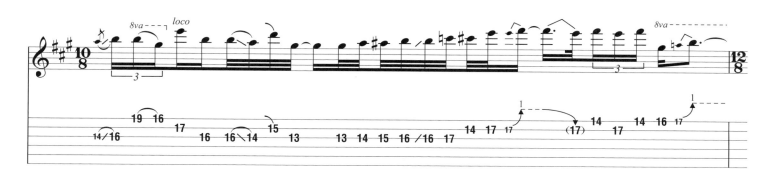

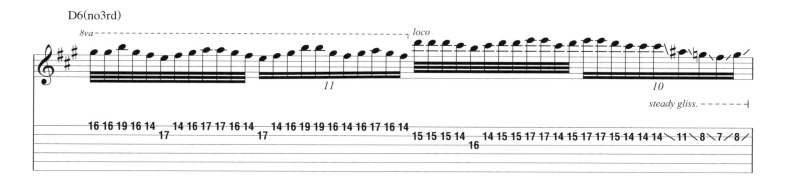

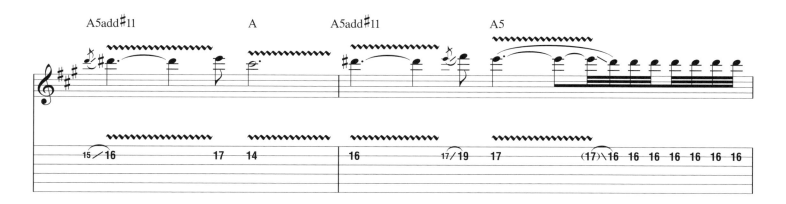

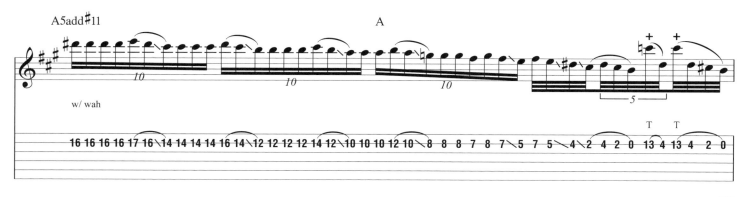

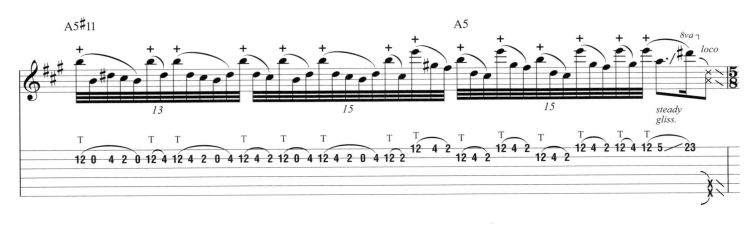

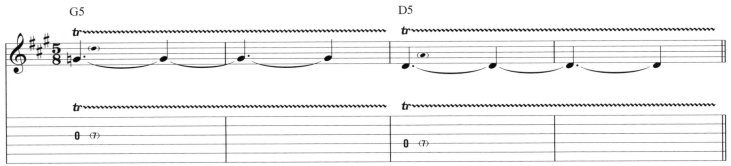

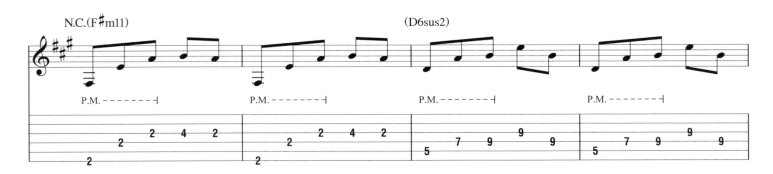

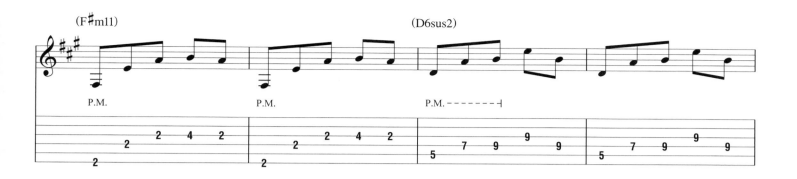

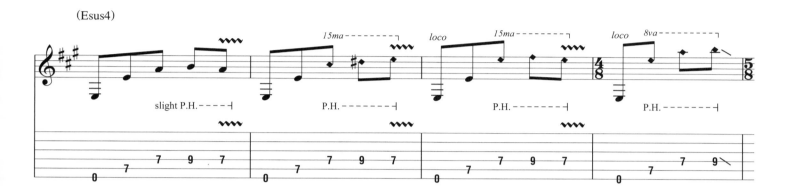

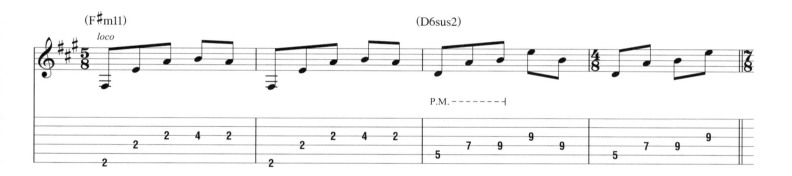

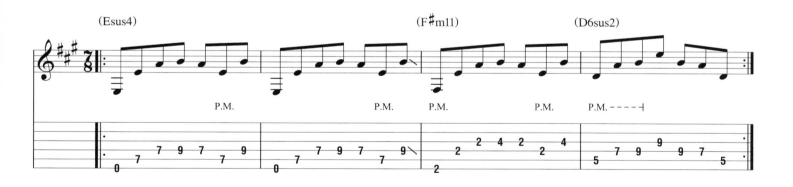

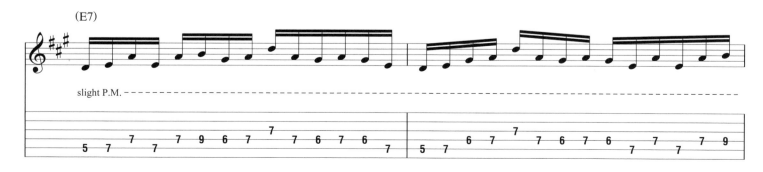

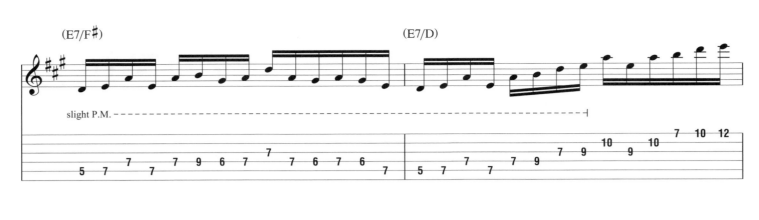

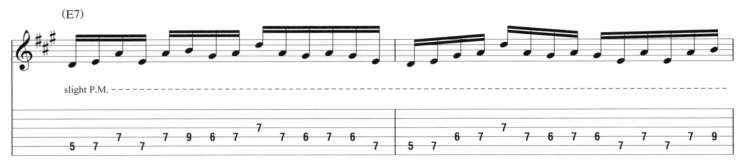

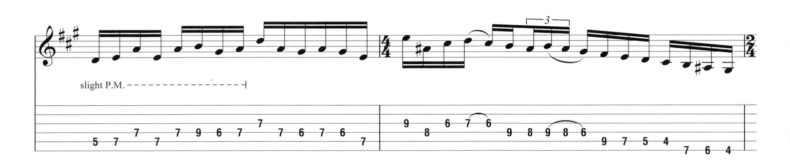

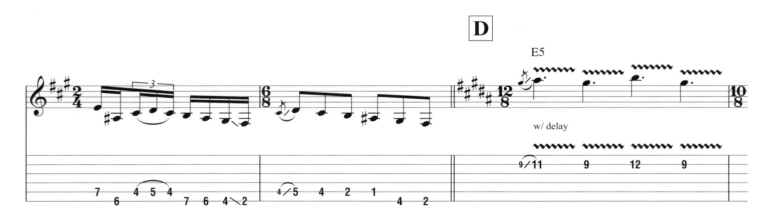

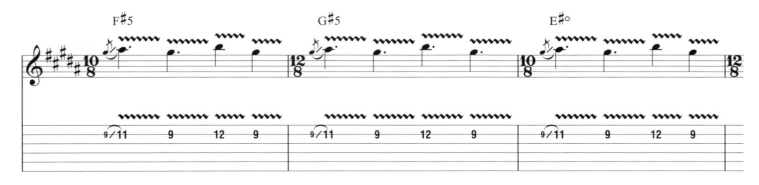

In the Presence of Enemies, Pt. 1

Music by John Petrucci, Mike Portnoy, John Myung, Kevin LaBrie and Jordan Rudess
Lyrics by John Petrucci

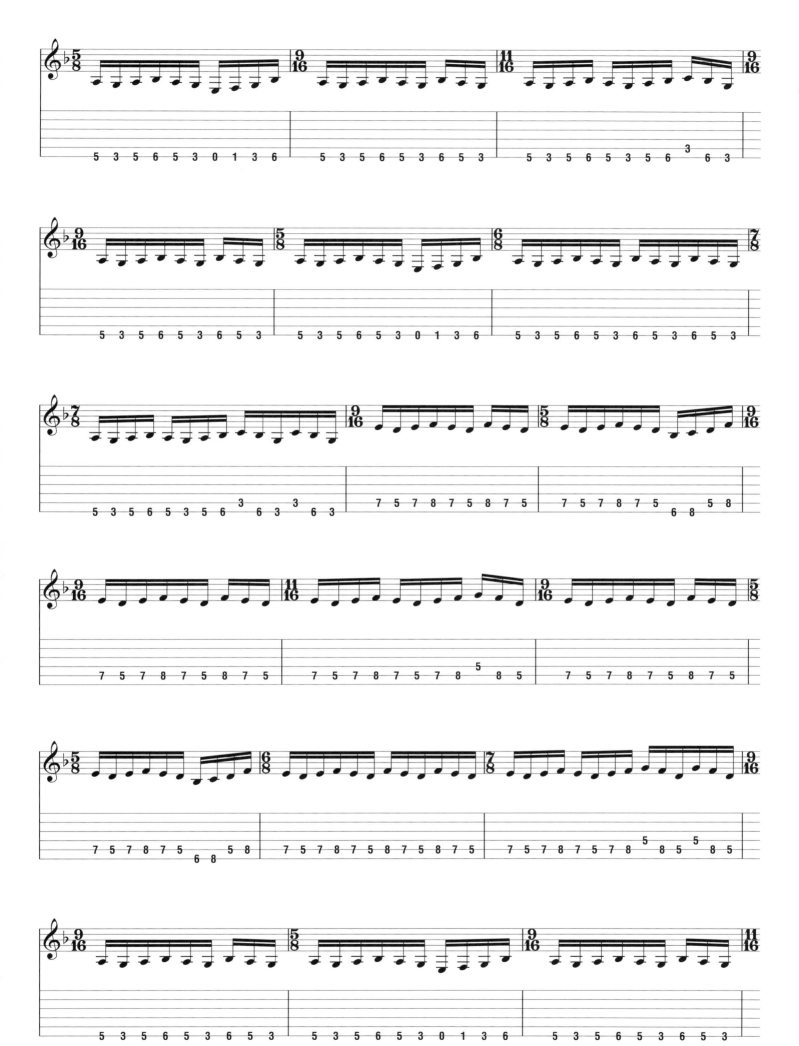

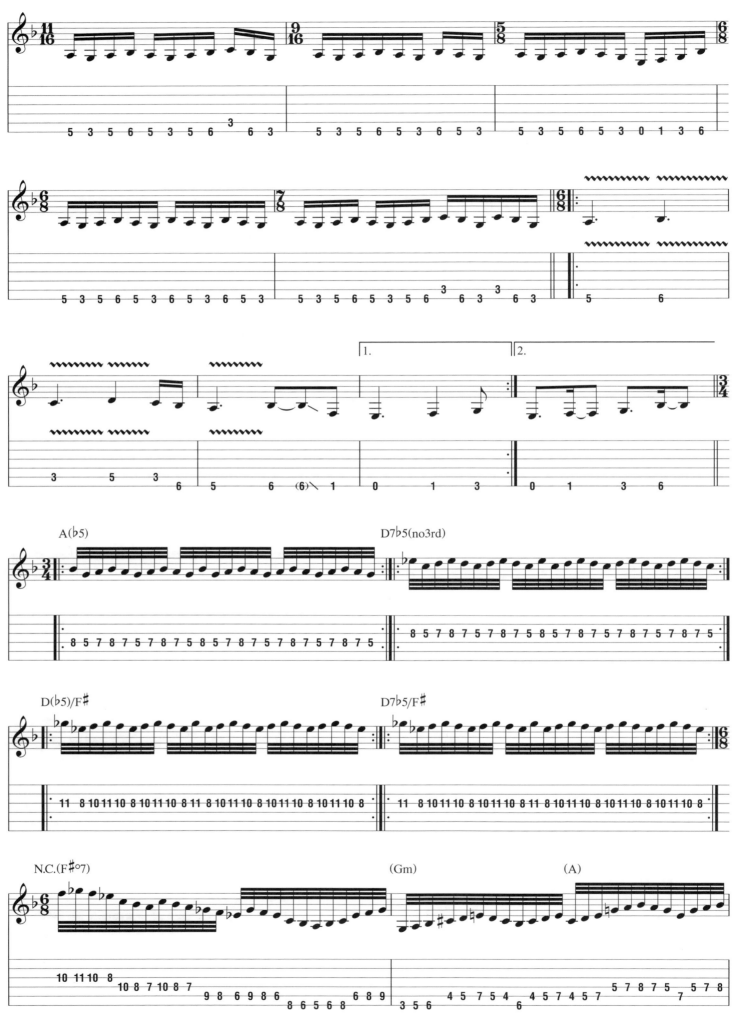

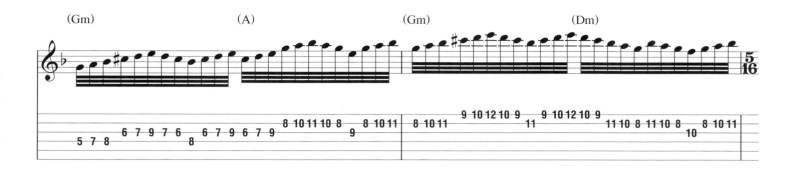

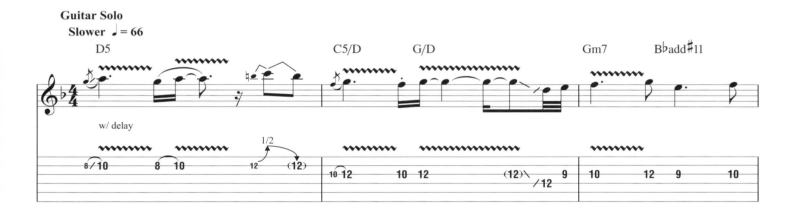

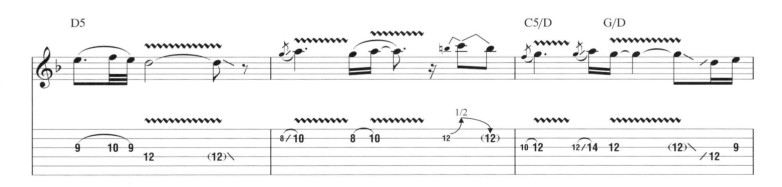

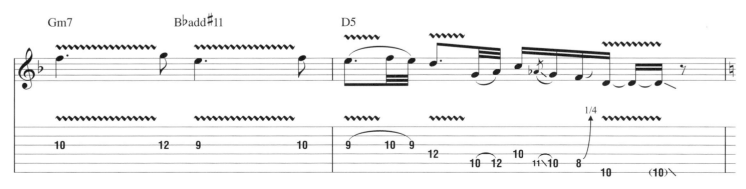

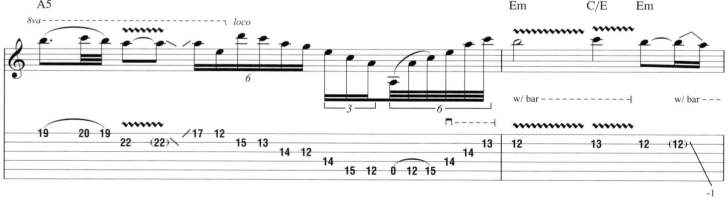

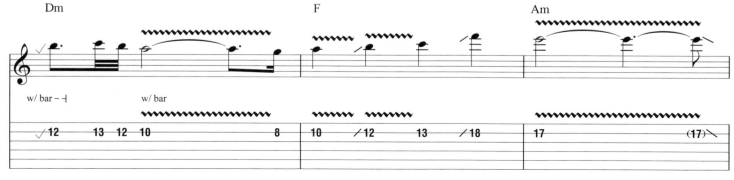

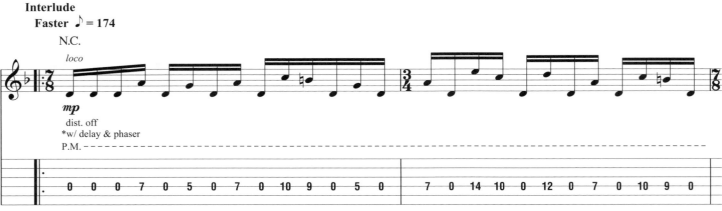

*Delay set for dotted eighth-note regeneration w/ 1 repeat.

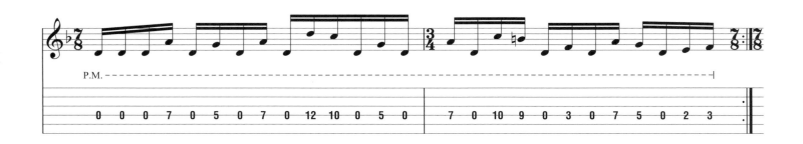

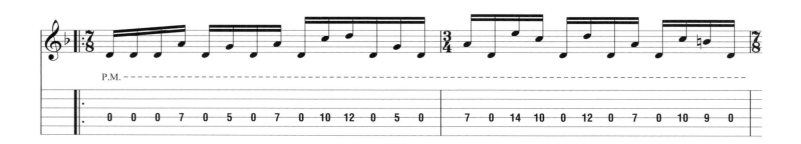

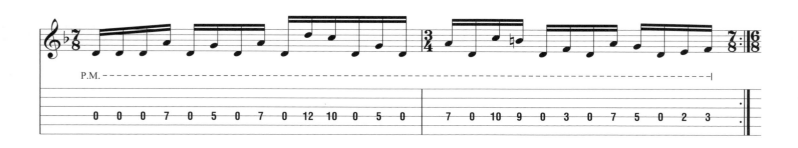

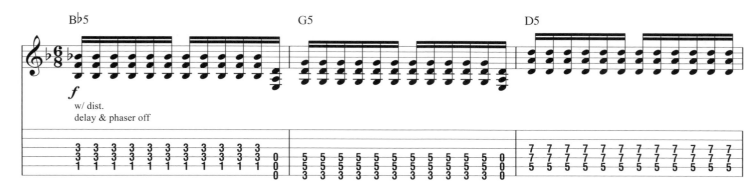

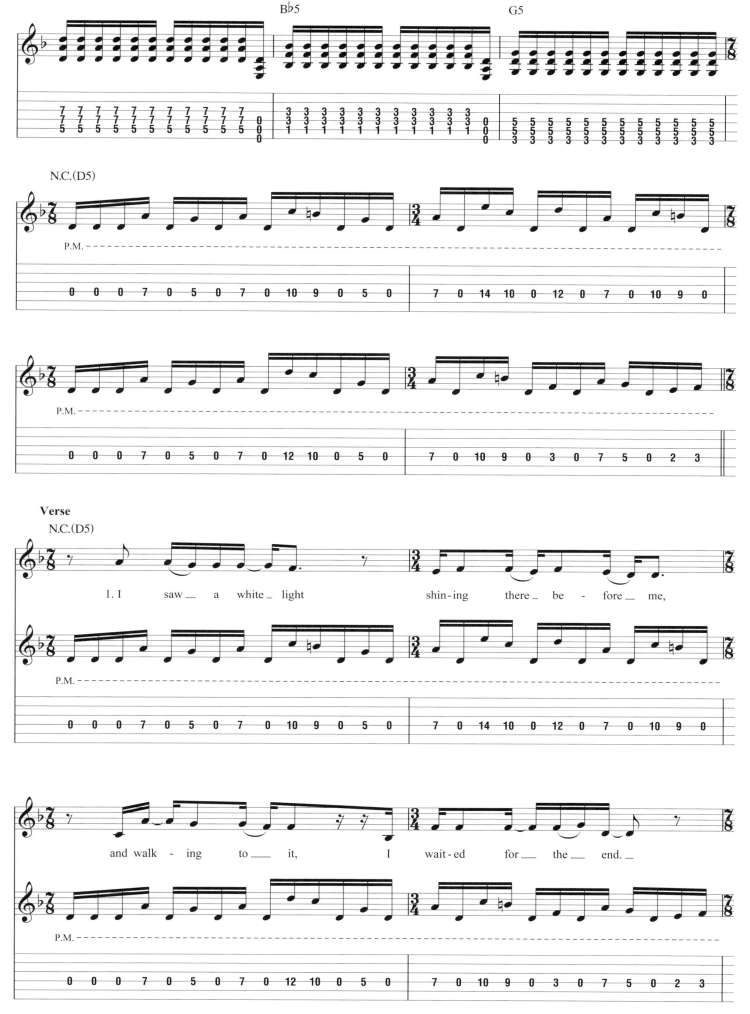

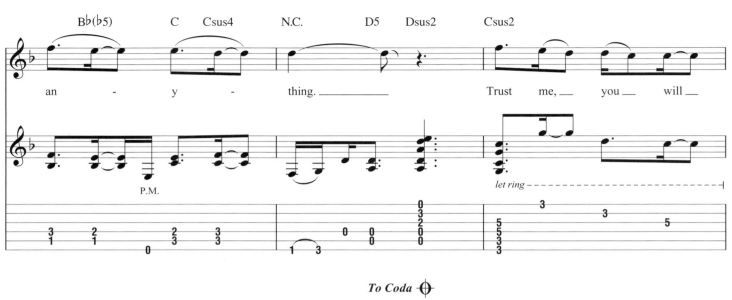

an - y - thing. _____ Trust me, _ you _ will _

To Coda ⊕

Interlude

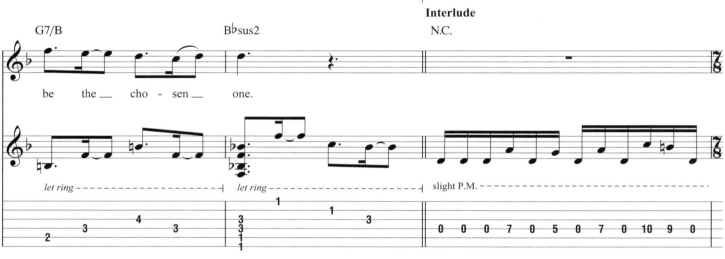

be the _ cho - sen _ one.

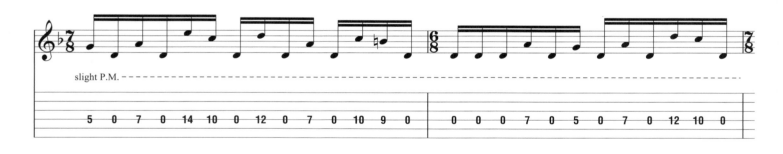

Verse

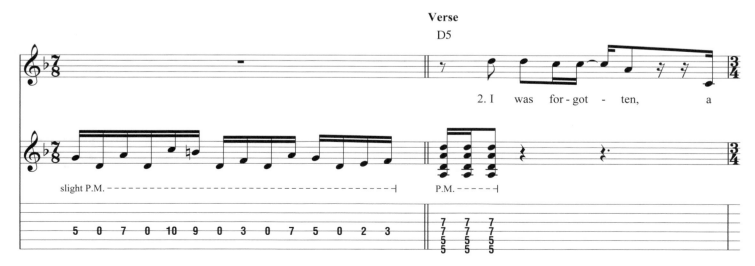

2. I was for - got - ten, a

bod - y scorned__ and bro - ken.   My soul__ re - ject - ed,

Bb5

taint - ed by ___ his blood. __   Be - yond _____ re - demp - tion,   a

G5   D5

sin - ner not ___ worth sav - ing.   For - ev - er tak - en

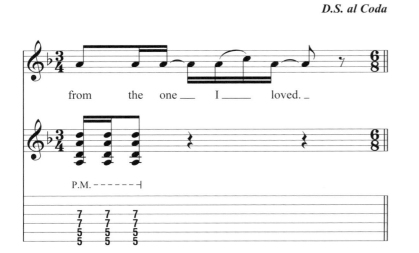

from   the   one ___ I ___ loved. __

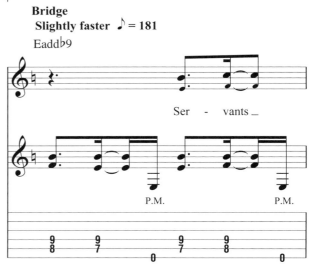

⊕ Coda

Bridge
Slightly faster ♪ = 181

Eadd♭9

D.S. al Coda

Ser - vants __

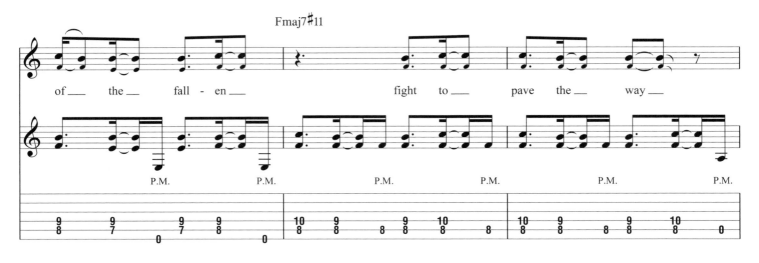

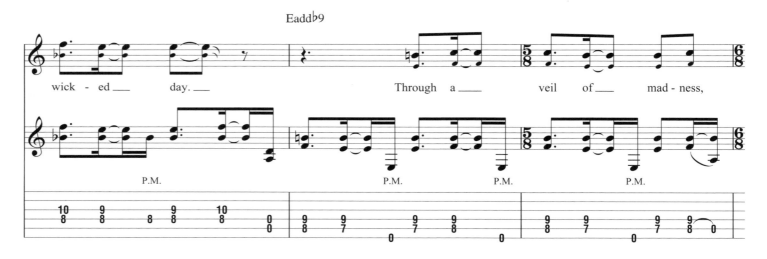

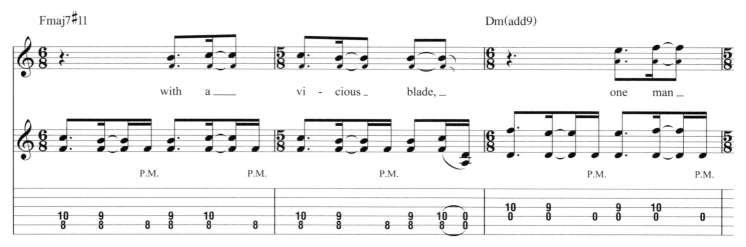

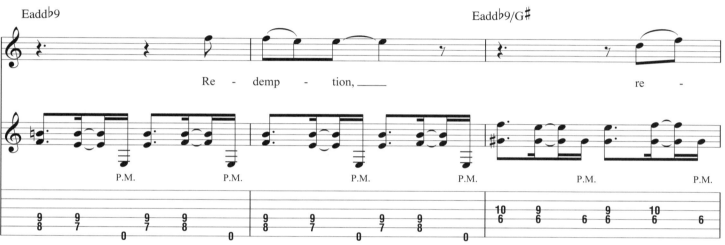

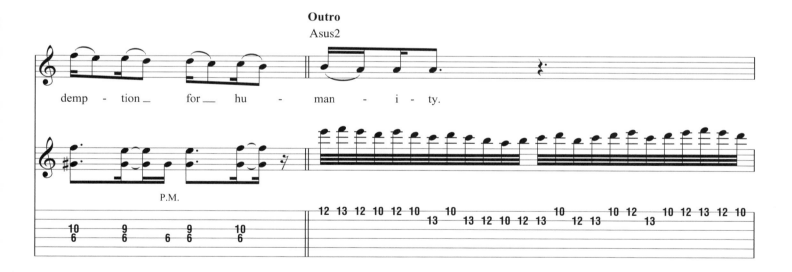

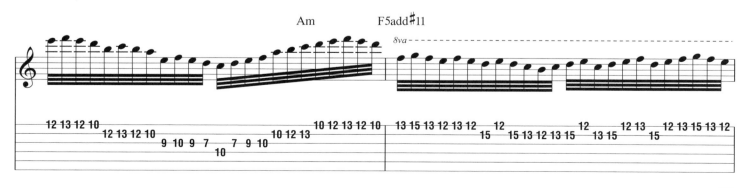

Dm(add9)

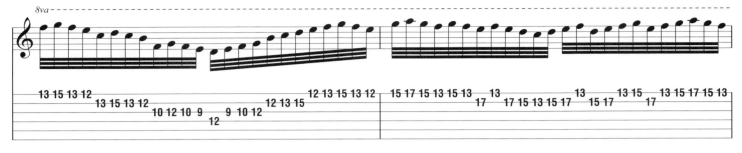

Eadd♭9/G♯

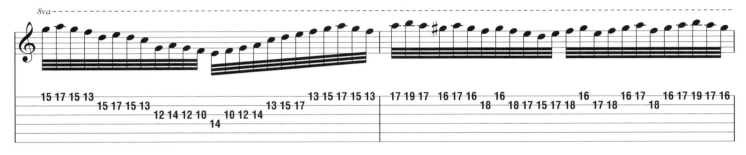

E5add♭9

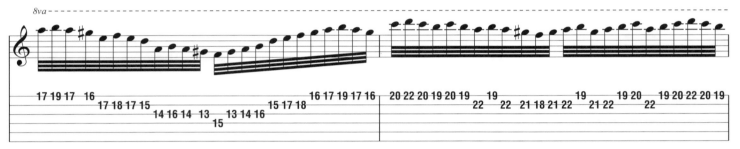

B♭5add♯11

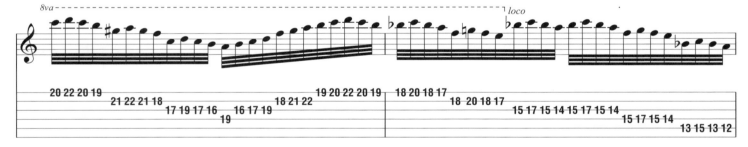

Bm

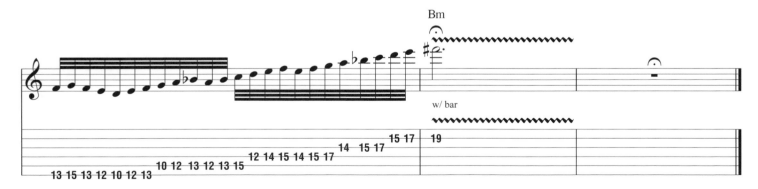

Additional Lyrics

Chorus Do I still wait for my god, and the symbol of my faith?
I can lead you down the path and back to life.
All I ask is that you worship me.
I can help you seek revenge and save yourself,
Give you life for all eternity.

Metropolis–Part 1
"The Miracle and the Sleeper"

Words and Music by Kevin LaBrie, Kevin Moore, John Myung, John Petrucci and Michael Portnoy

*Delay set for quarter-note regeneration, slightly lower volume than dry signal.

84

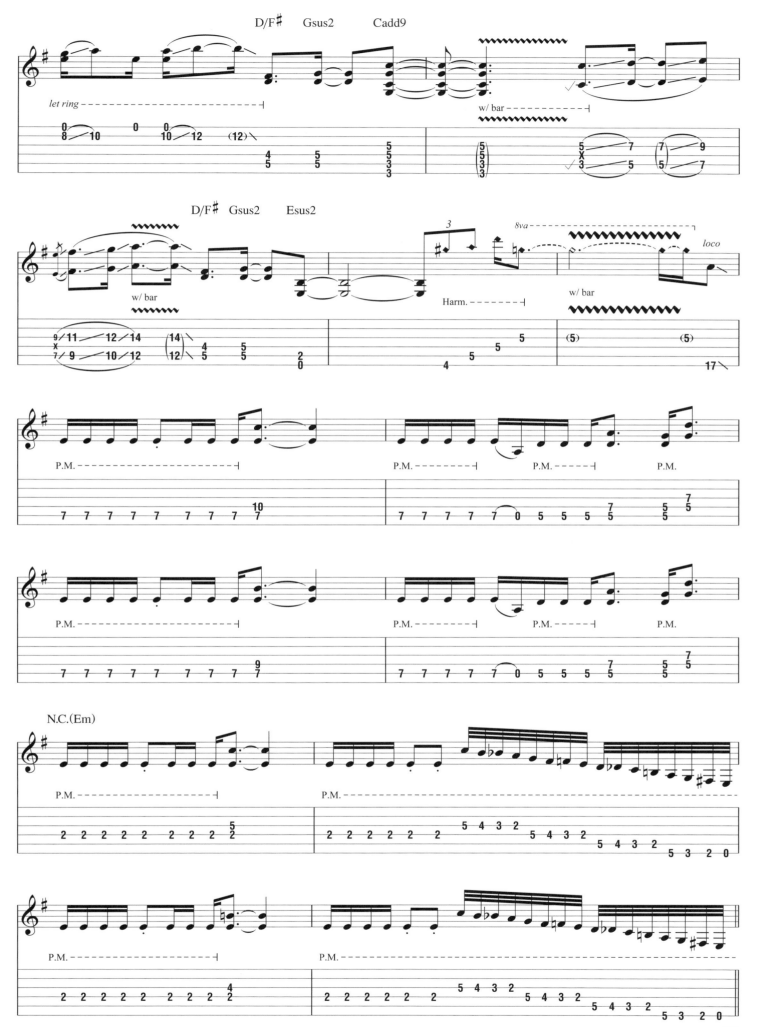

Verse

1. The smile of ___ dawn _____ ar - rived ear - ly May. _____ She car - ried a gift from her home. _____ The night shed a tear to

Bm   G/B   Em/B

As a man, I've found it's all caught up with me. I'm a-

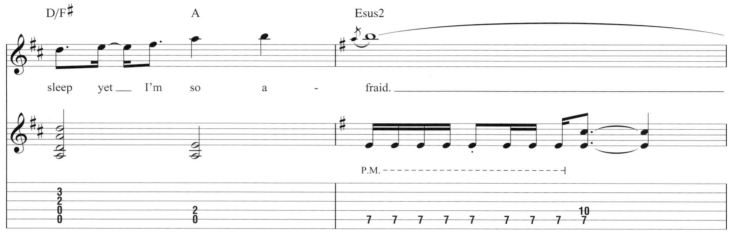

D/F♯   A   Esus2

sleep yet I'm so a - fraid.

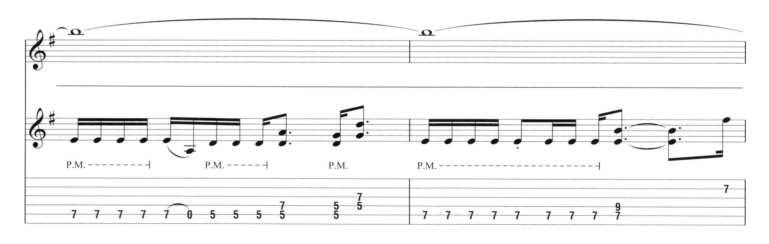

Verse

D/F♯   Gsus2   Cadd9/E

3. Some - where, like a

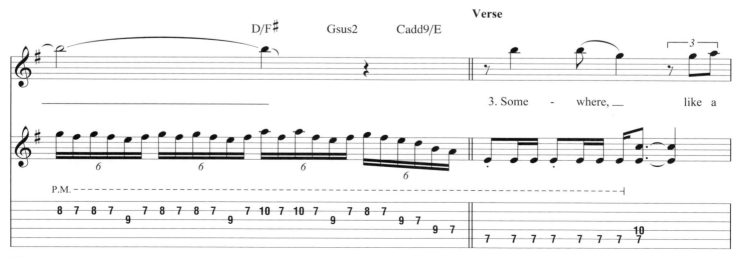

90

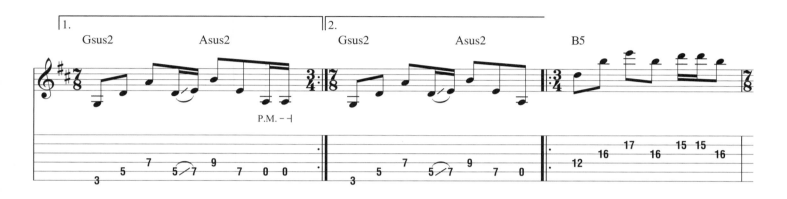

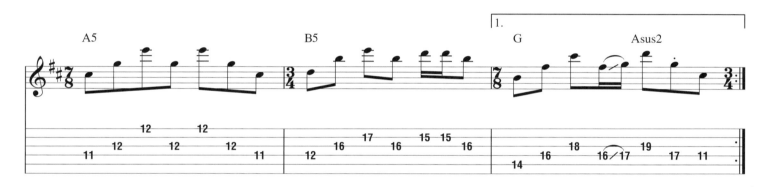

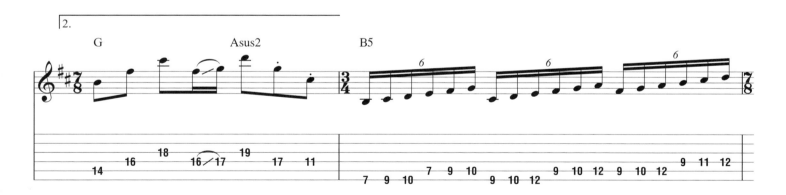

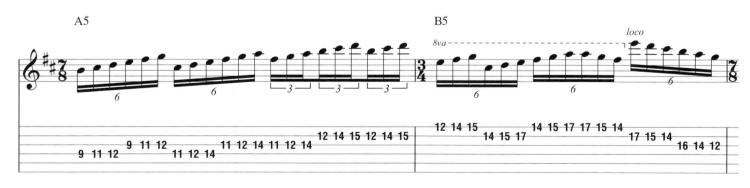

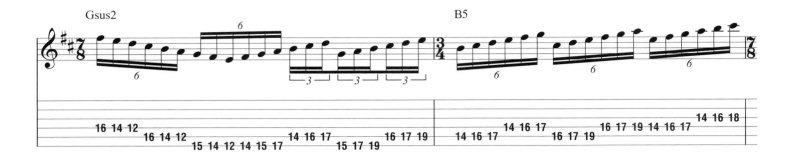

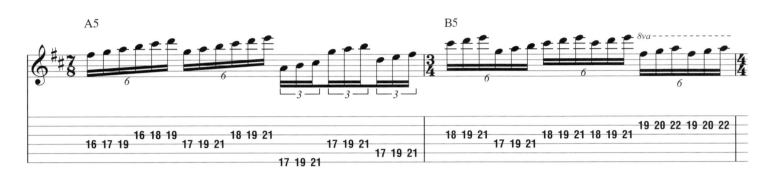

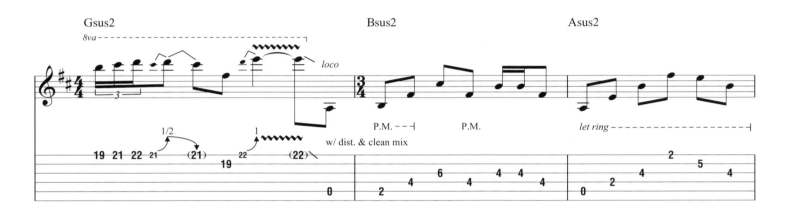

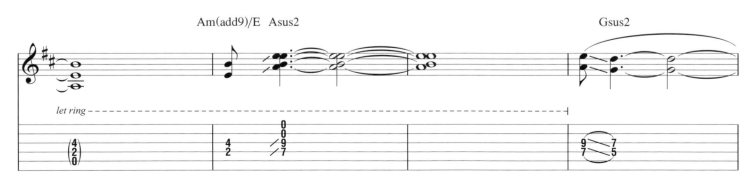

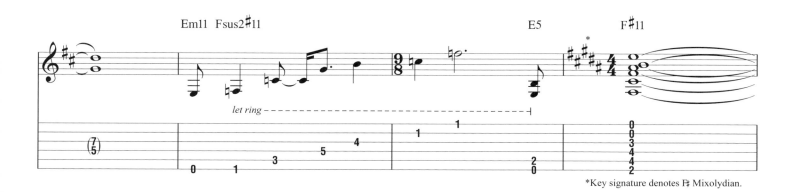

Em11 Fsus2#11

E5 F#11

*Key signature denotes F# Mixolydian.

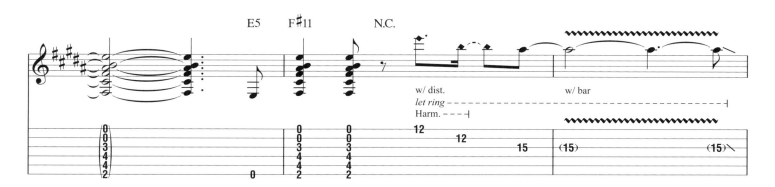

E5 F#11

N.C.

w/ dist.

w/ bar

let ring

Harm.

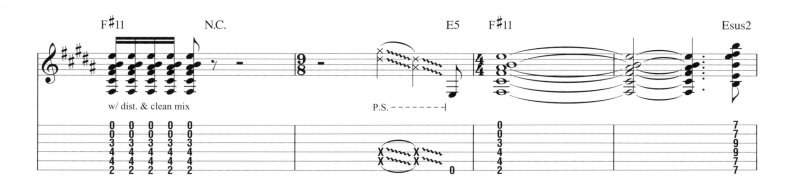

F#11

N.C.

E5 F#11

Esus2

w/ dist. & clean mix

P.S.

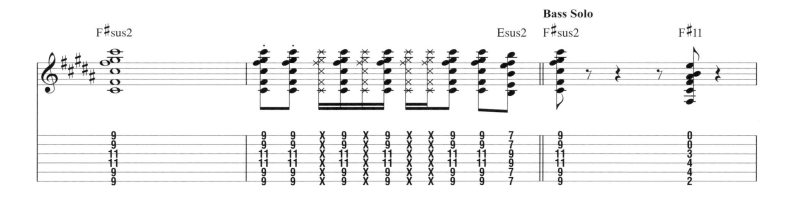

F#sus2

Bass Solo

Esus2 F#sus2

F#11

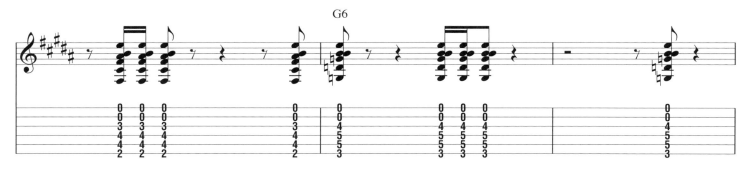

G6

Double-time feel

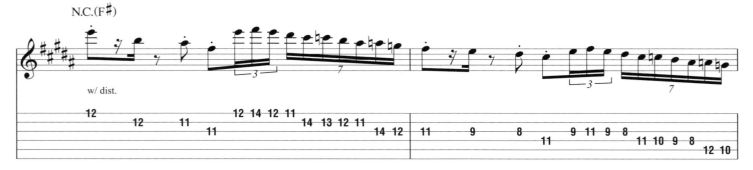

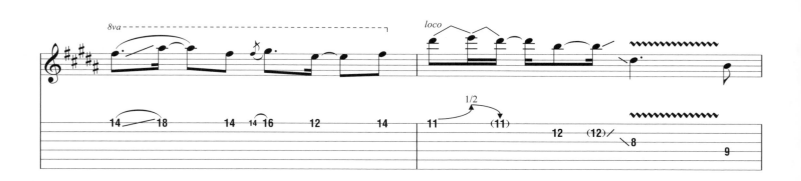

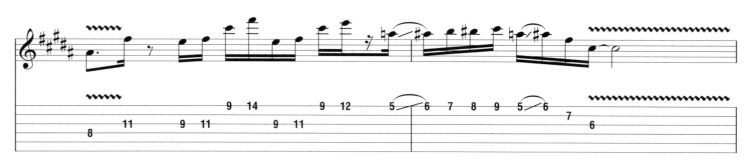

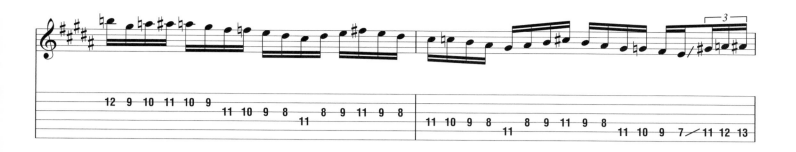

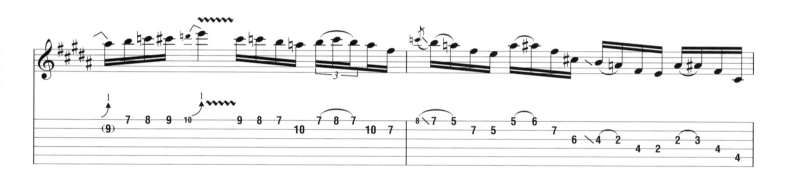

End double-time feel

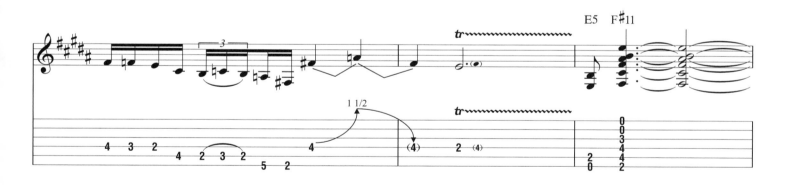

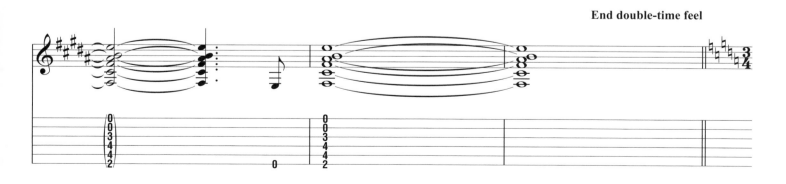

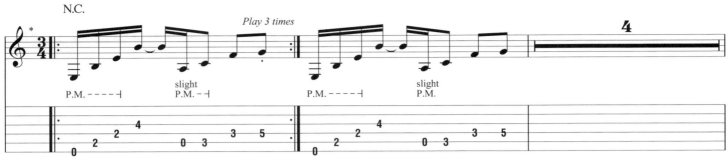

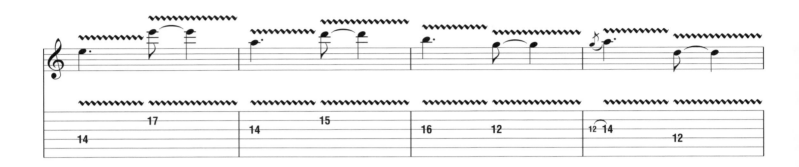

*Key signature denotes E Phrygian.

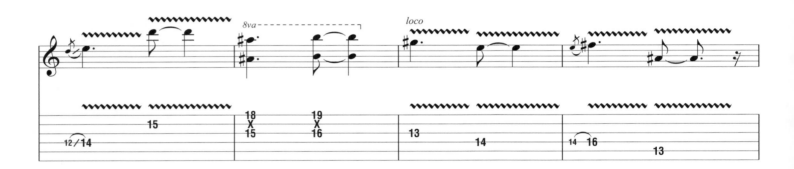

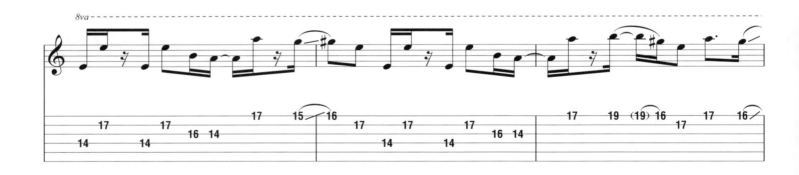

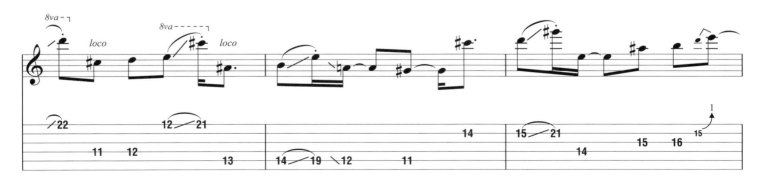

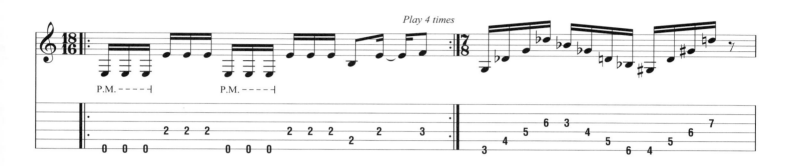

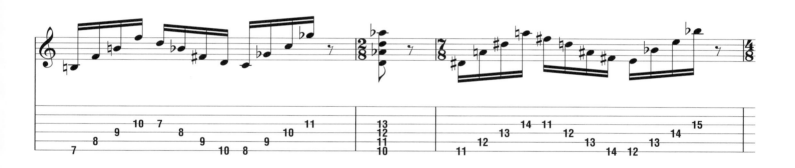

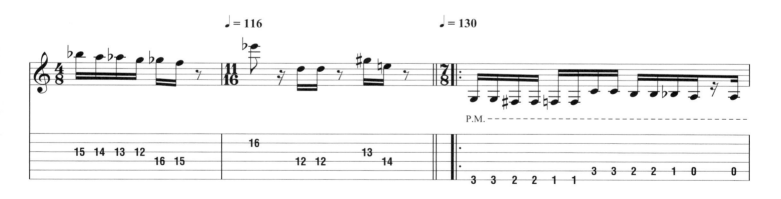

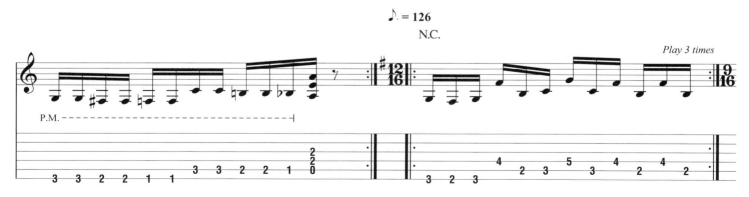

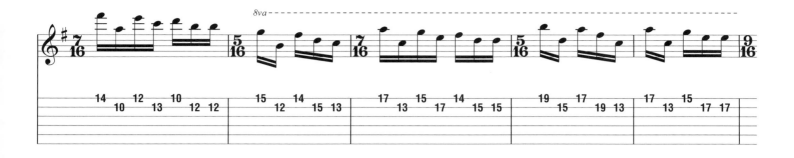

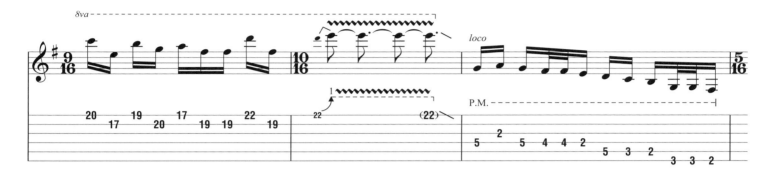

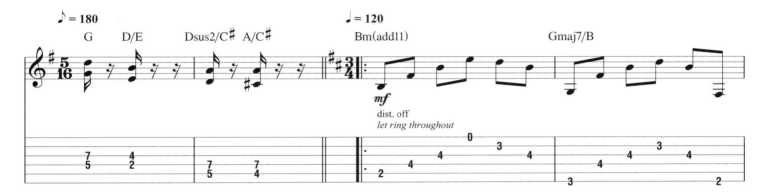

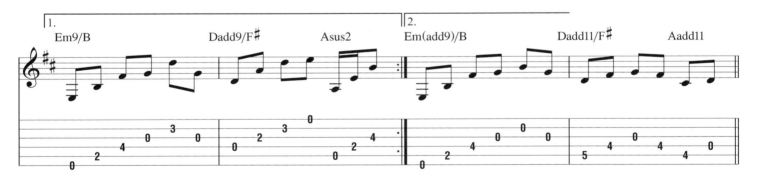

Outro

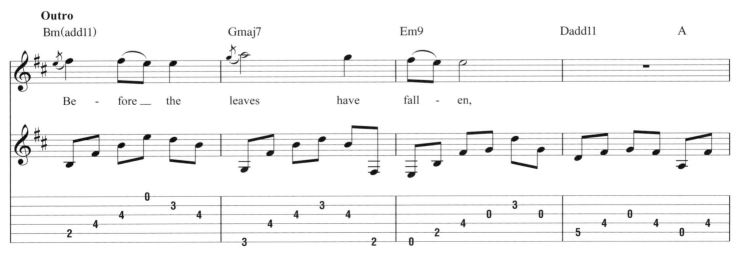

Be - fore __ the leaves have fall - en,

On the Backs of Angels

Music by John Petrucci, John Myung and Jordan Rudess
Lyrics by John Petrucci

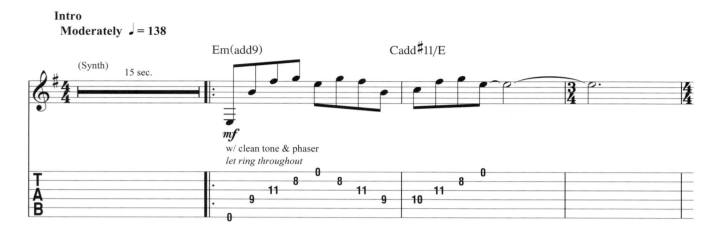

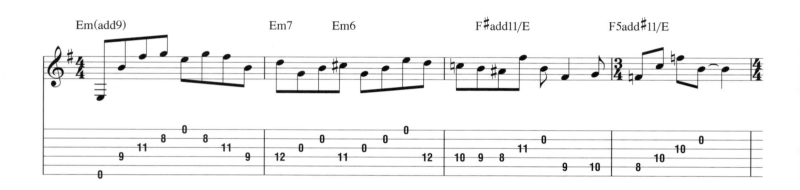

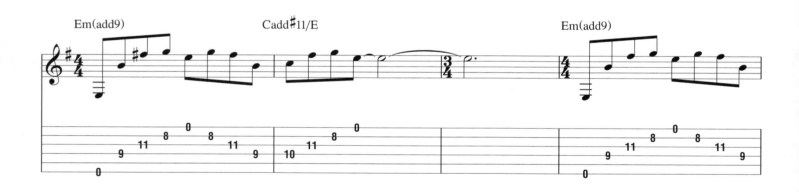

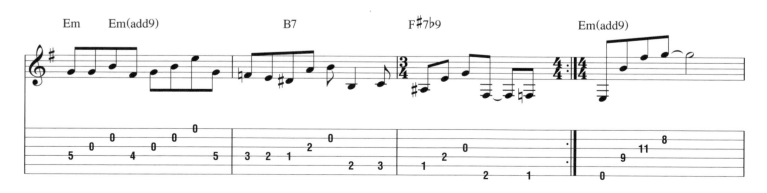

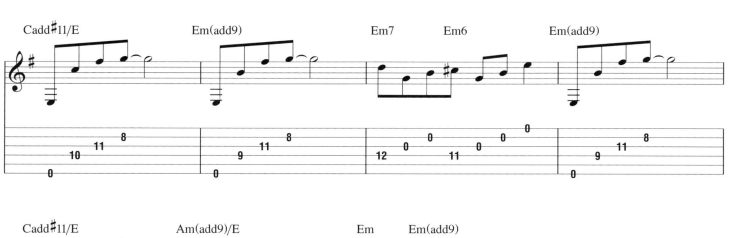

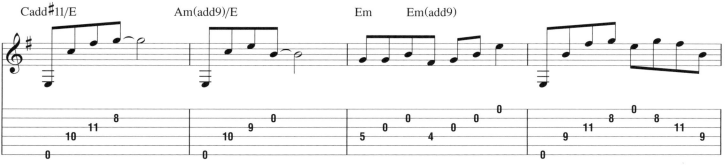

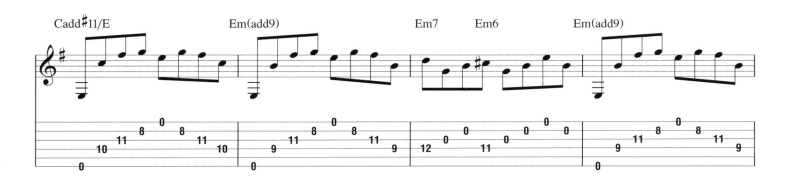

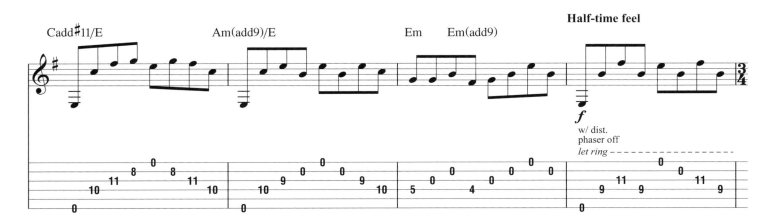

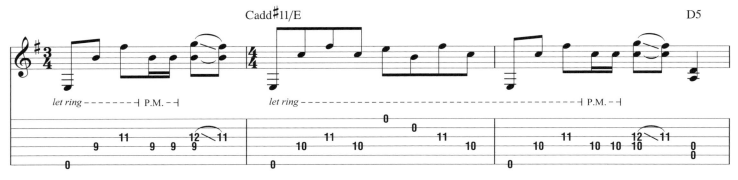

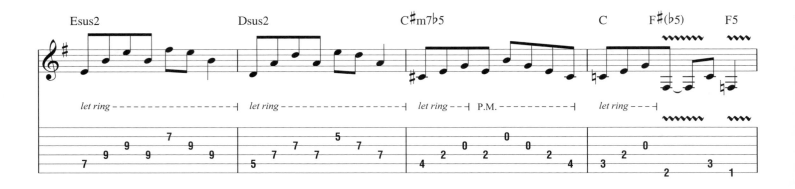

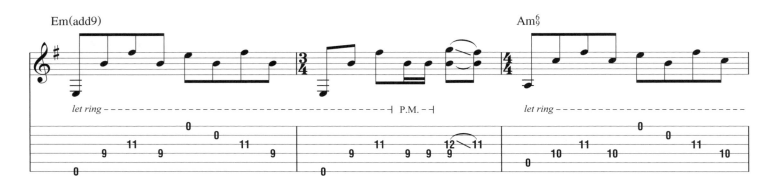

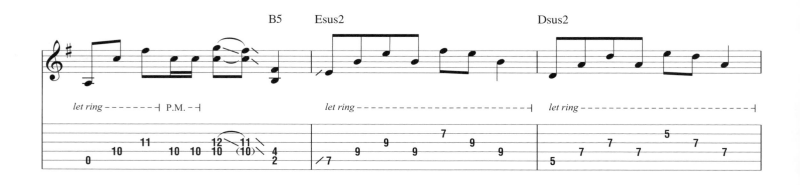

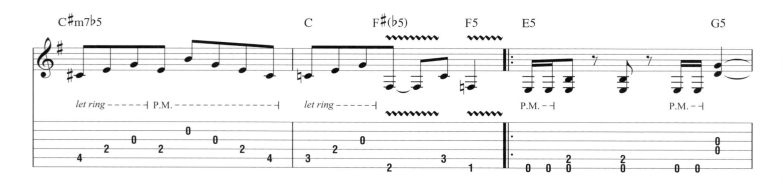

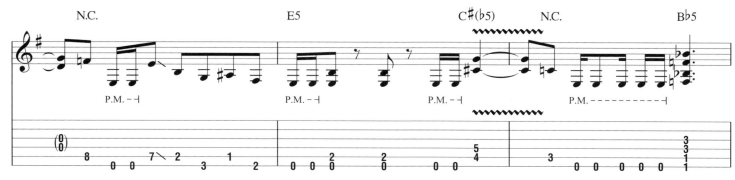

1st time, end half-time feel

Play 3 times

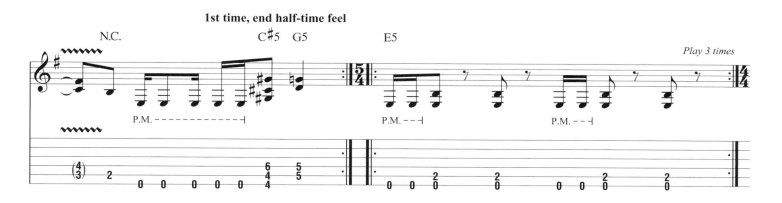

Verse
Half-time feel

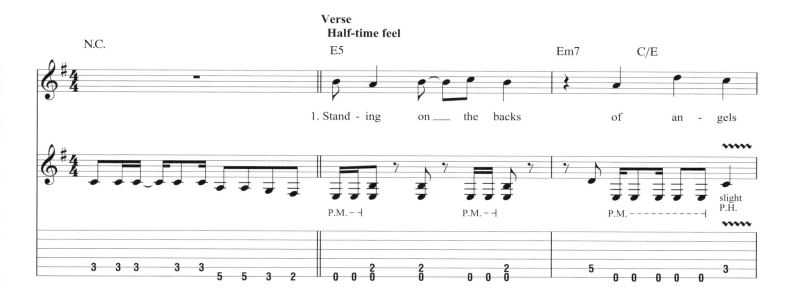

1. Stand - ing on ___ the backs of an - gels

des - ti - ned to ___ cre - ate. Mount - ing the ___ at - tack

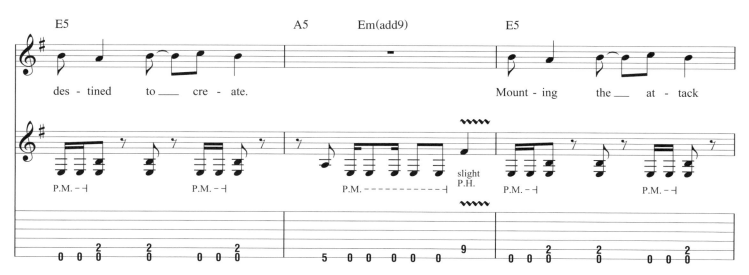

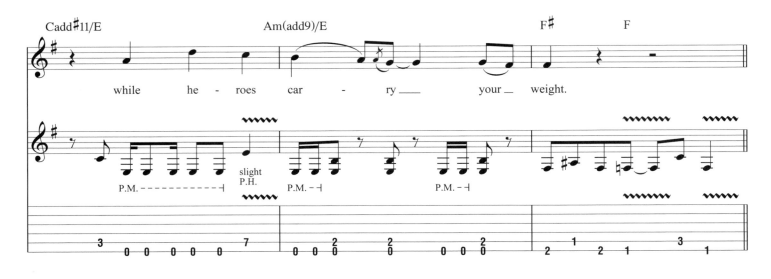

while he - roes car - ry ___ your __ weight.

Pre-Chorus

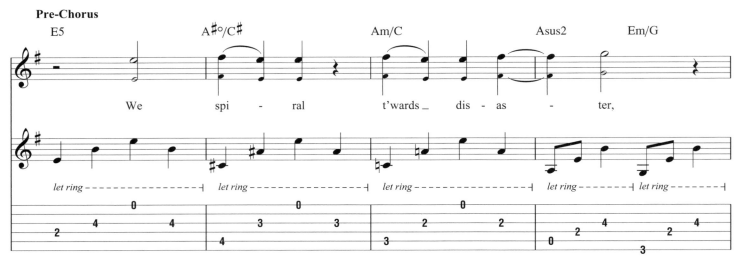

We spi - ral t'wards __ dis - as - ter,

End half-time feel

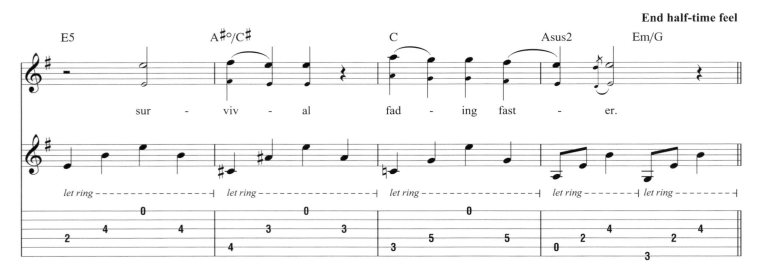

sur - viv - al fad - ing fast - er.

Interlude

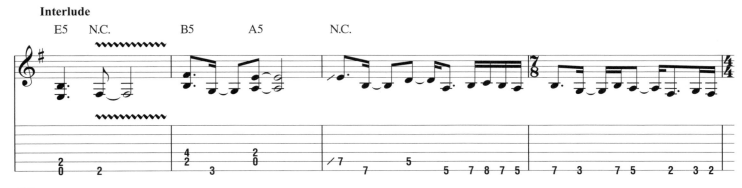

Interlude

Half-time feel

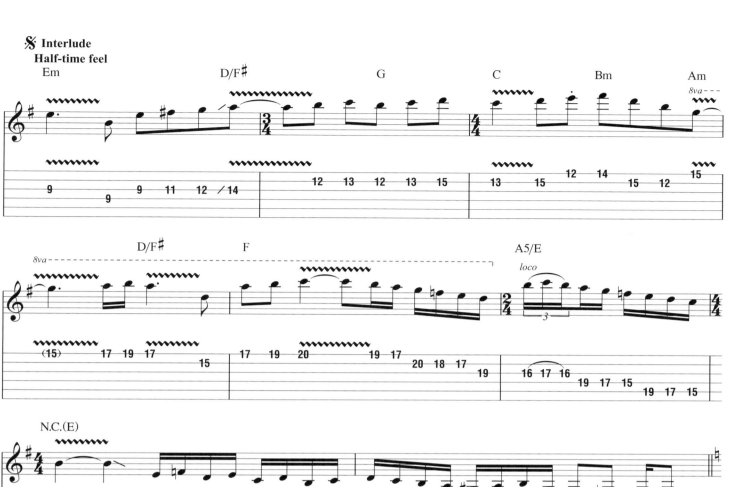

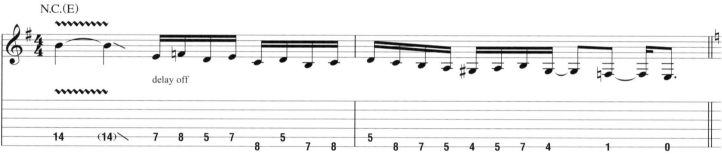

Chorus

3rd time, substitute Fill 2

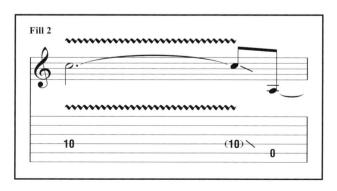

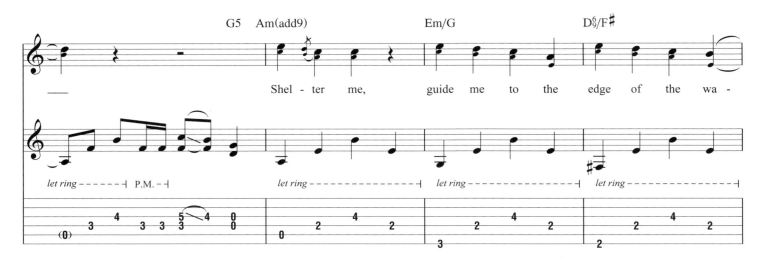

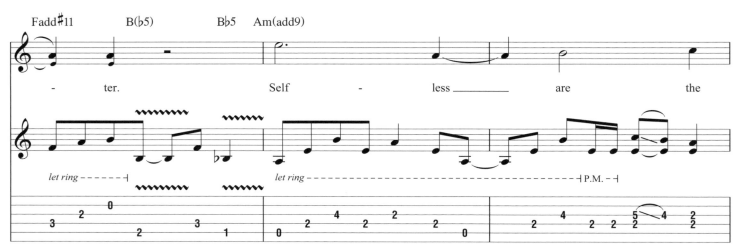

2nd time, substitute Fill 1
3rd time, substitute Fill 3

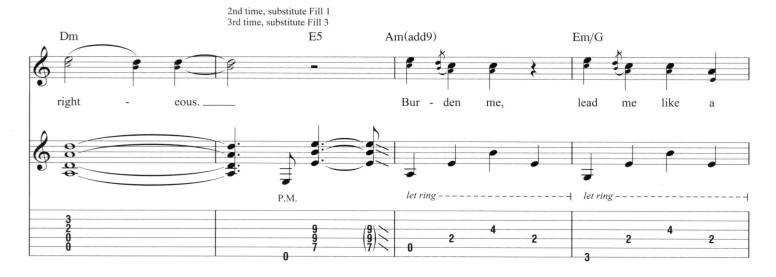

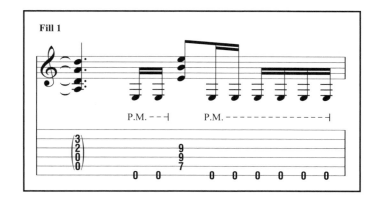

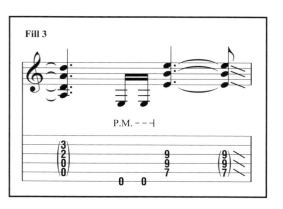

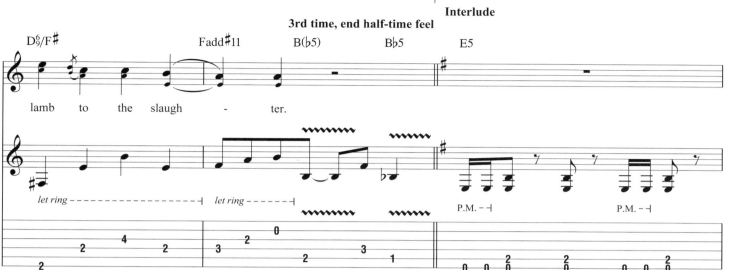

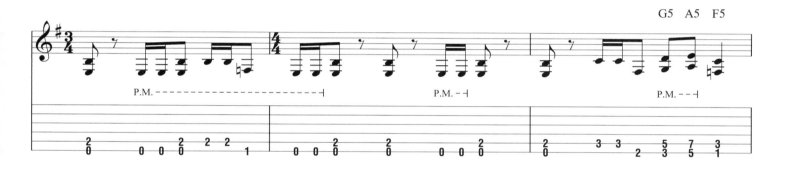

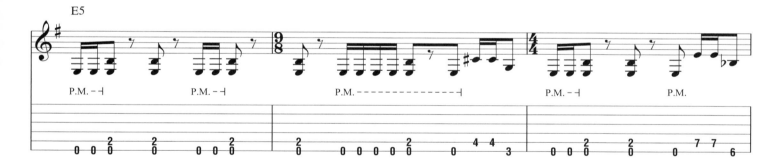

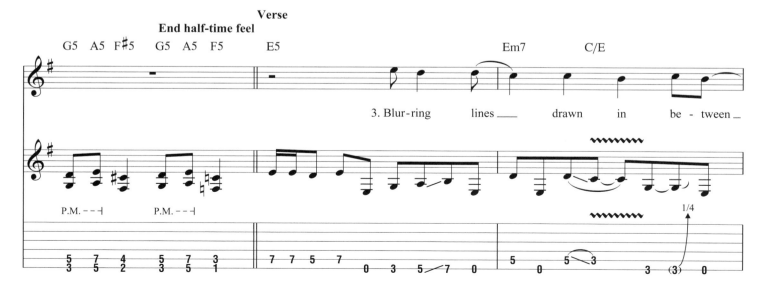

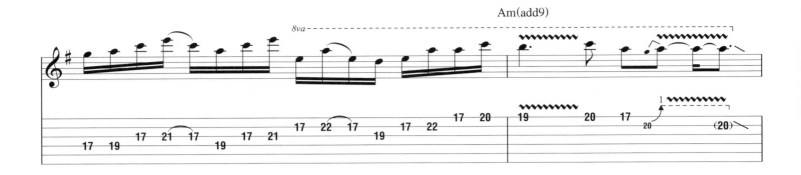

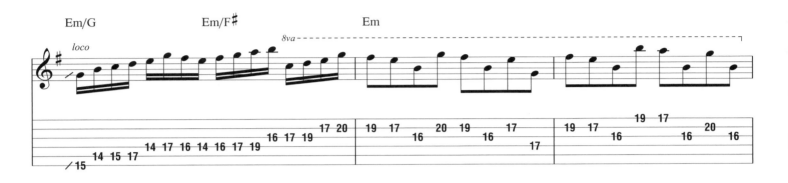

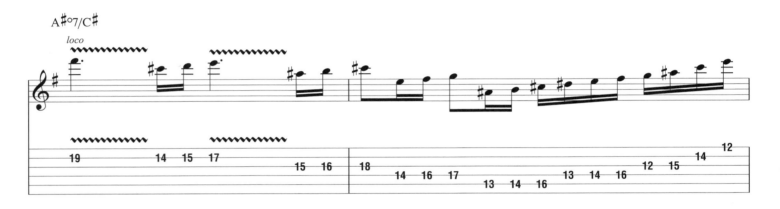

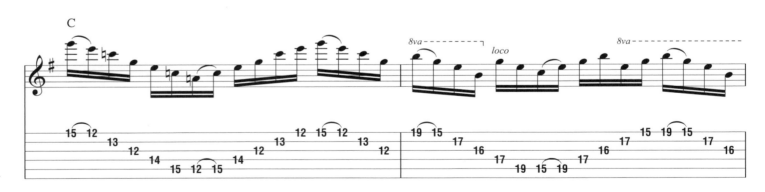

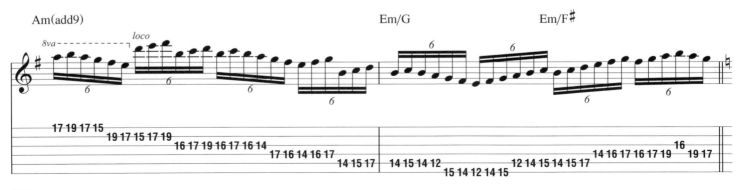

Interlude

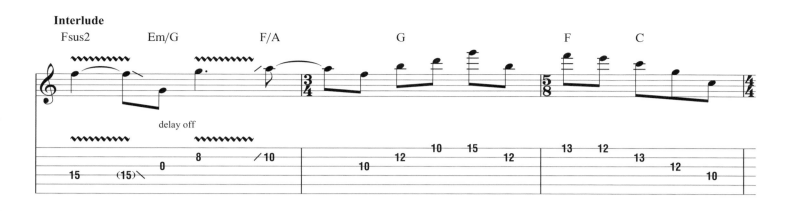

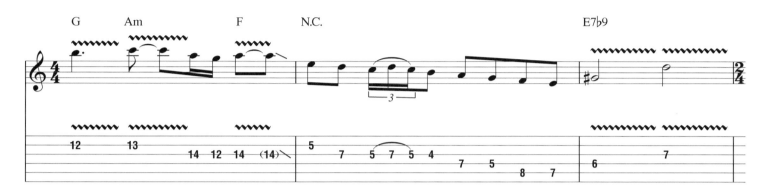

D.S.S. al Coda 2

Coda 2

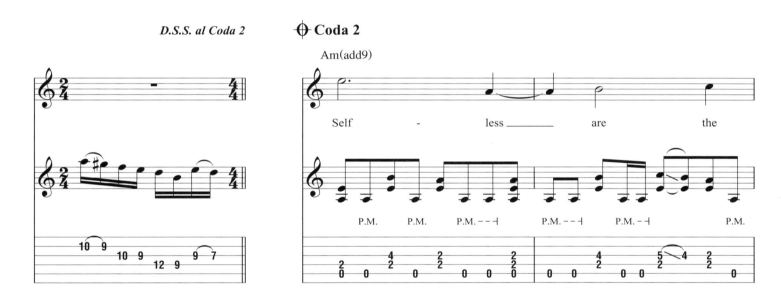

Self - less _____ are the

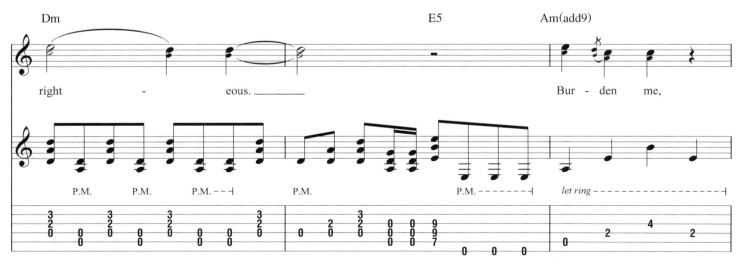

right - eous. _____ Bur - den me,

117

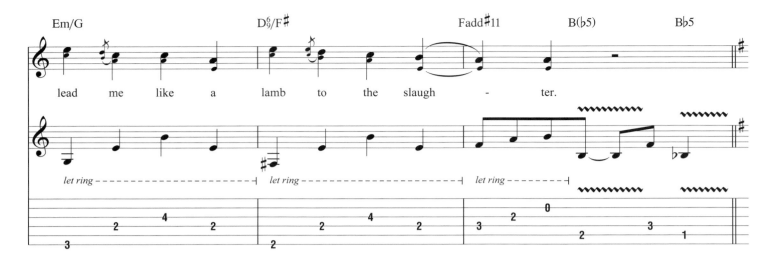

lead me like a lamb to the slaugh - ter.

Interlude
Half-time feel

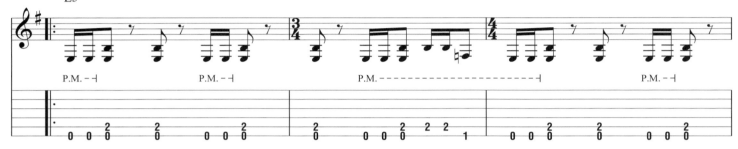

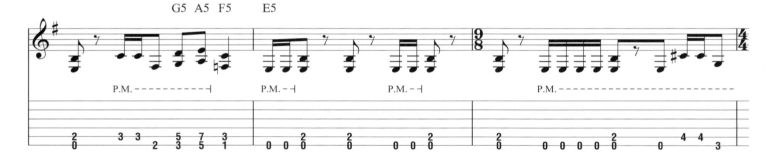

Outro
2nd time, end half-time feel

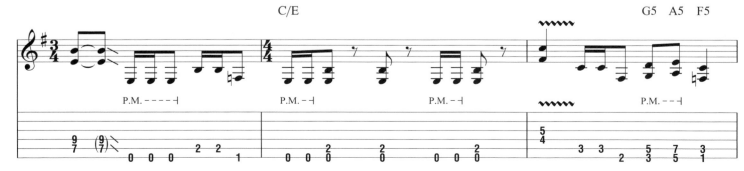

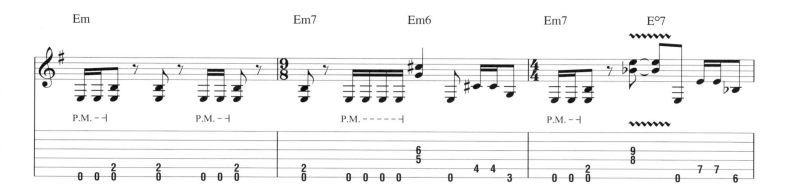

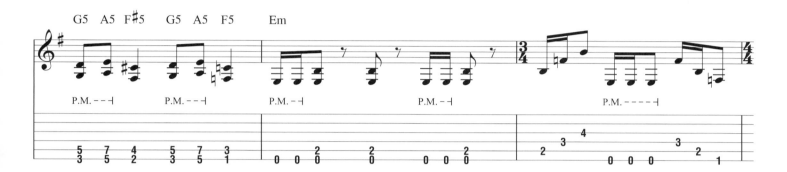

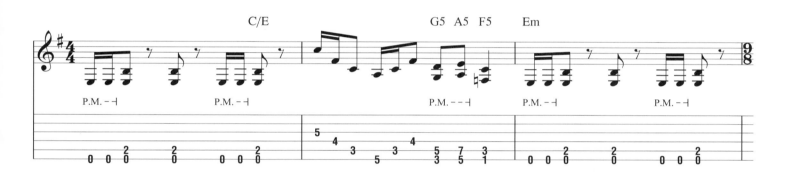

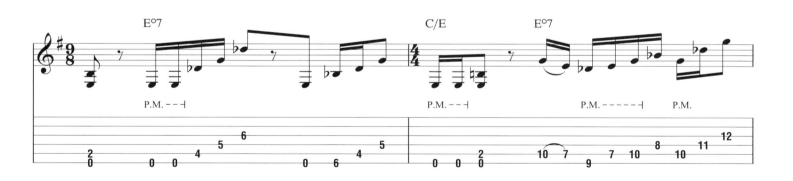

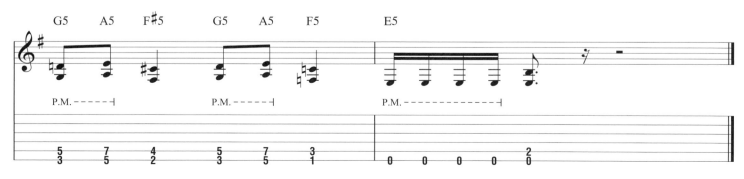

Six Degrees of Inner Turbulence: I. Overture

Music by John Petrucci, Michael Portnoy, John Myung and Jordan Rudess

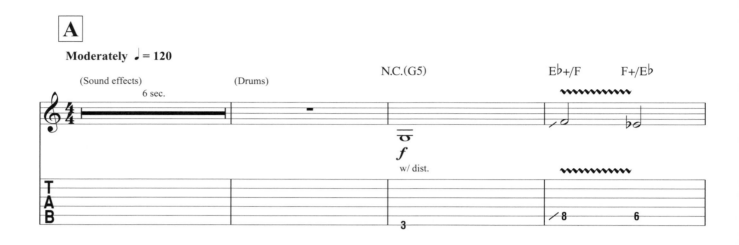

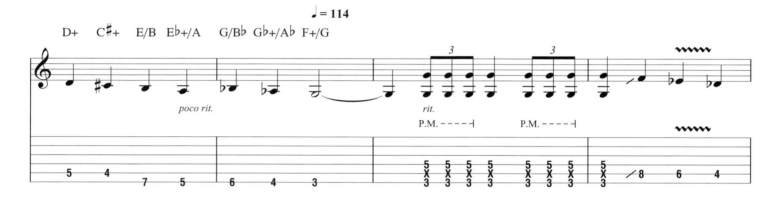

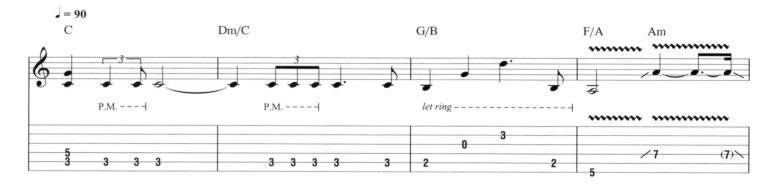

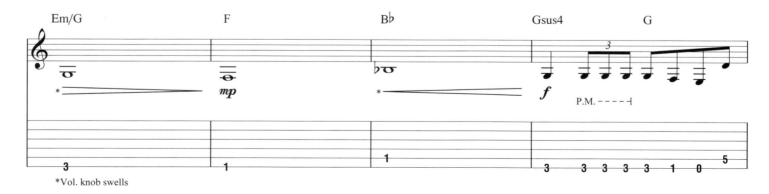

*Vol. knob swells

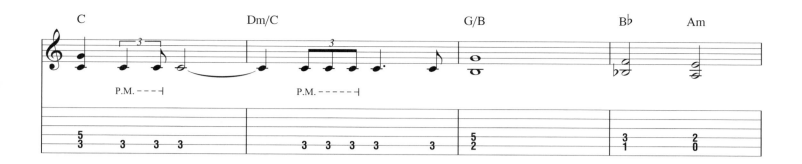

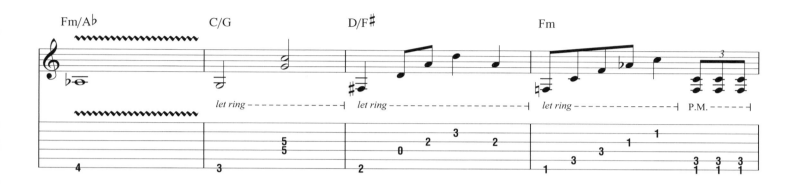

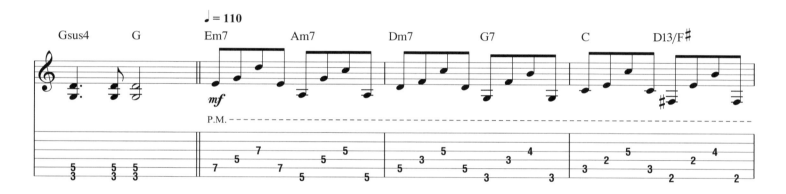

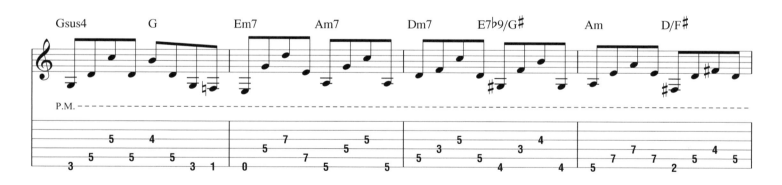

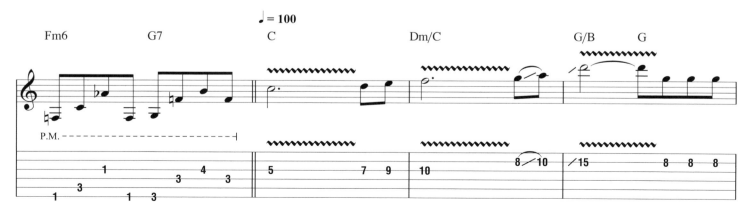

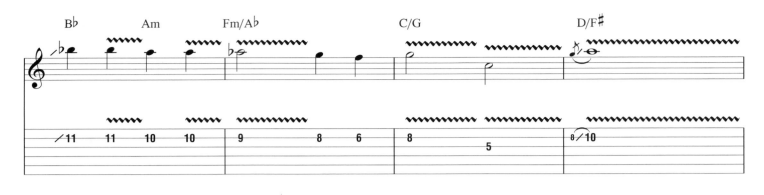

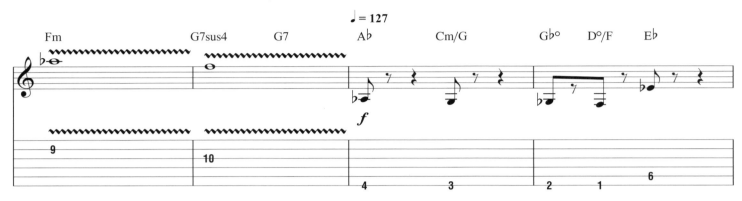

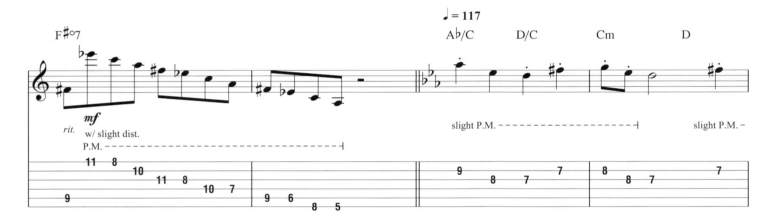

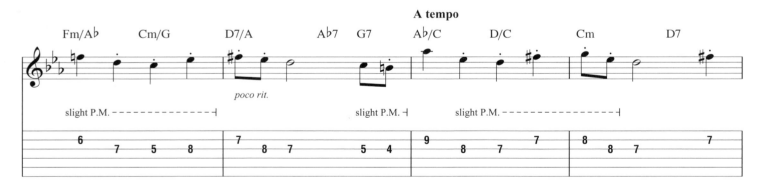

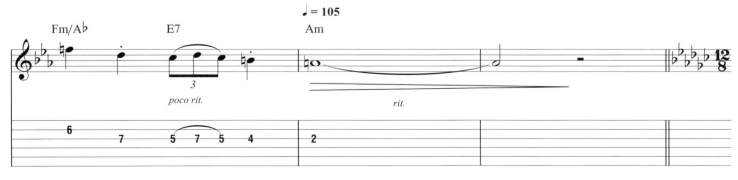

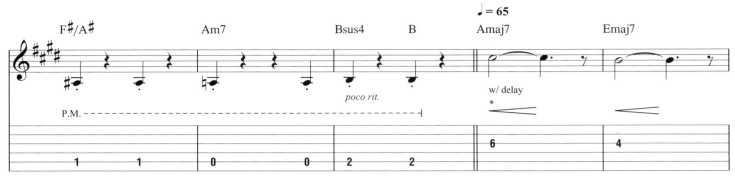

*Swells w/ vol. pedal, next 8 meas.

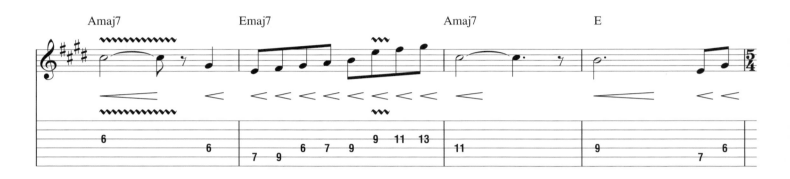

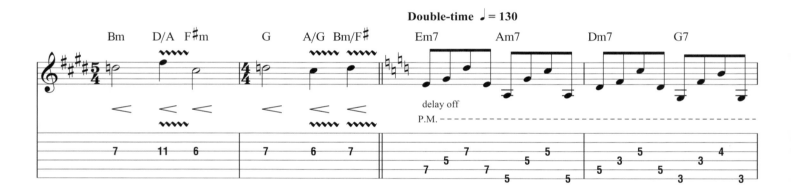

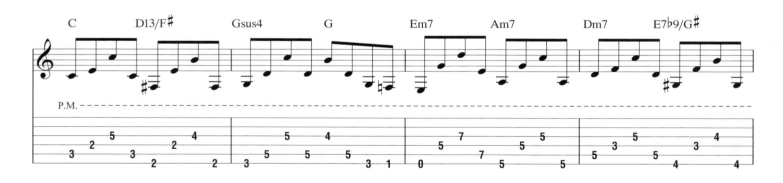

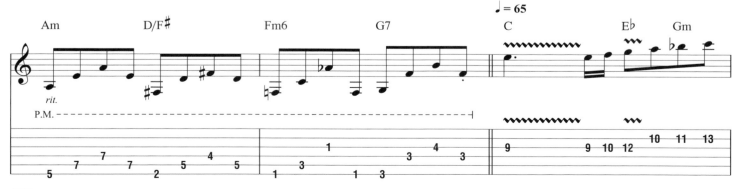

Segue to "II. About to Crash"

Six Degrees of Inner Turbulence:
II. About to Crash

Words and Music by John Petrucci, Michael Portnoy, John Myung and Jordan Rudess

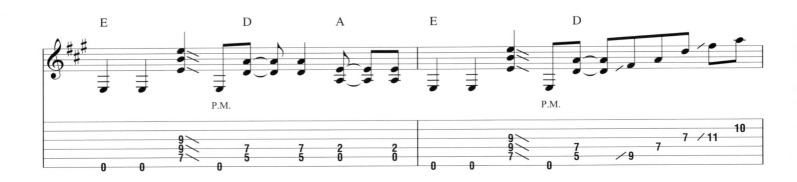

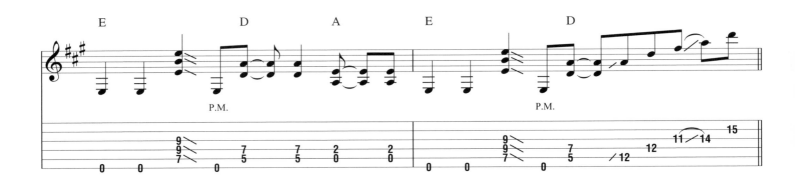

Verse

1. She can't stop pac - ing, _____ she nev - er felt _ so a - live.

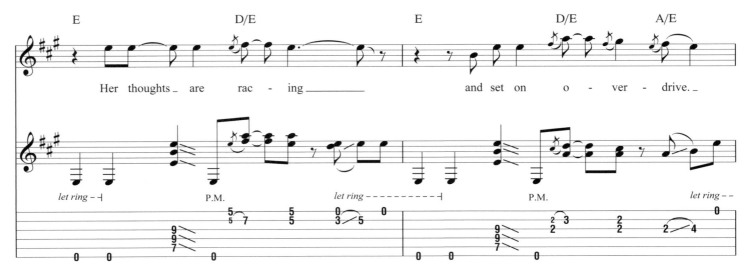

Her thoughts _ are rac - ing _____ and set on o - ver - drive. _

130

*Key signature denotes B Mixolydian.

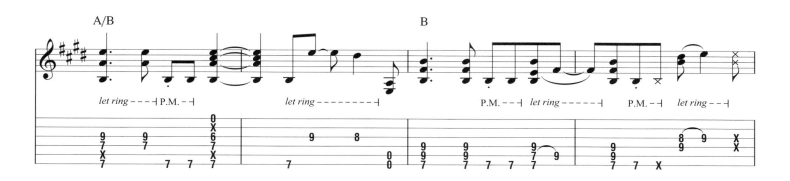

Verse

2. She was raised _ in a small _

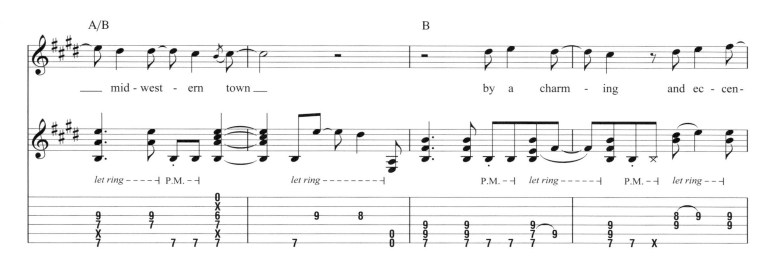

_ mid-west-ern town _ by a charm-ing and ec-cen-

-tric lov-ing fa- ther. She was praised _ as the per-

133

*Key signature denotes E Mixolydian.

138

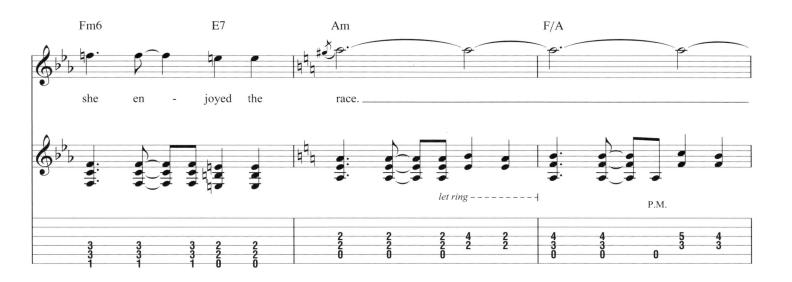

she en - joyed the race.

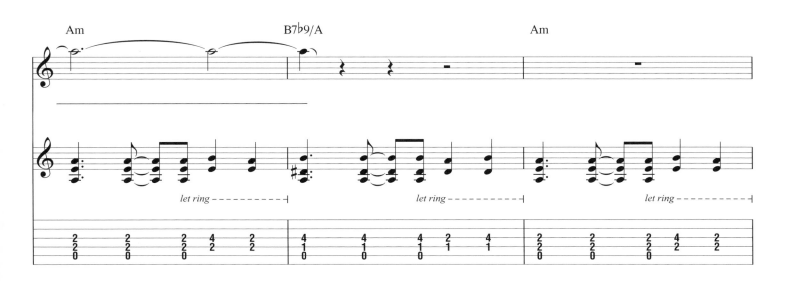

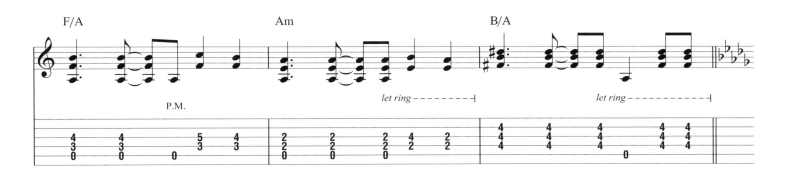

Guitar Solo

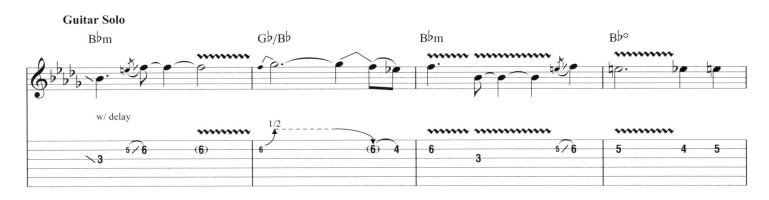

*Release bend while diving w/ bar.

140

Under a Glass Moon

Words and Music by Kevin LaBrie, Kevin Moore, John Myung, John Petrucci and Michael Portnoy

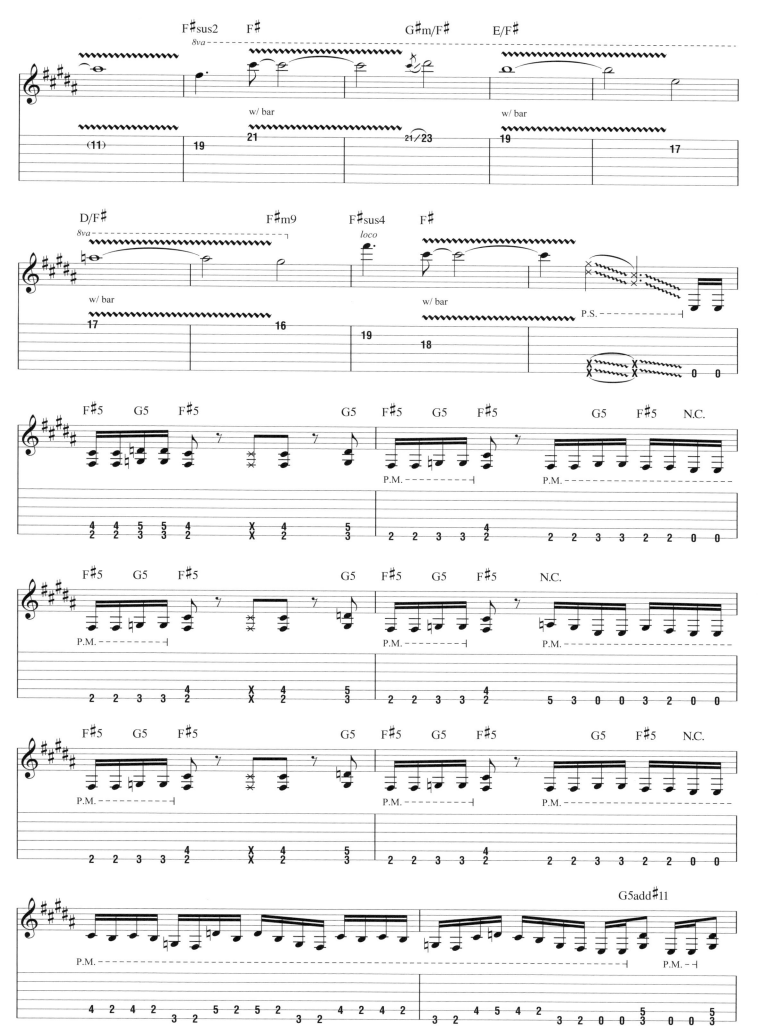

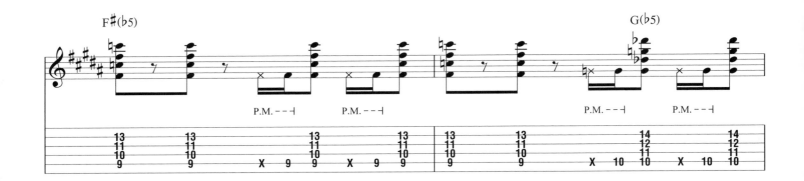
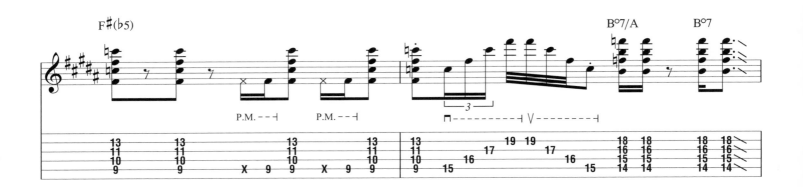
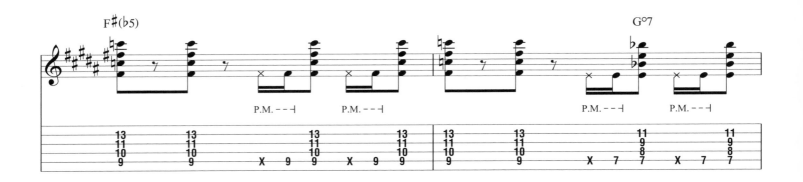
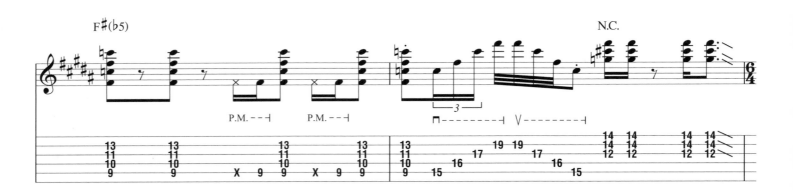

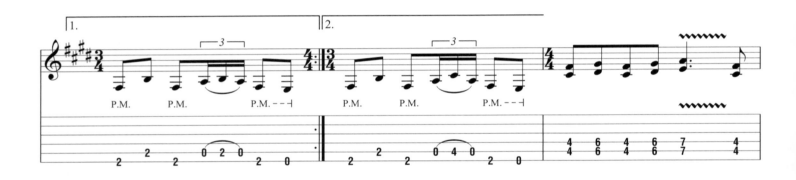

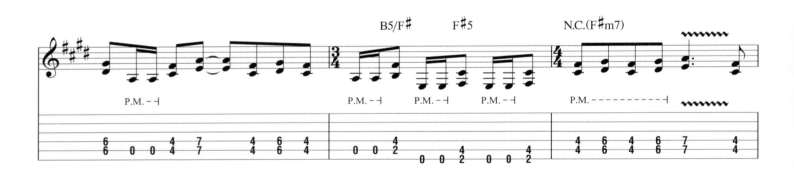

Guitar Solo

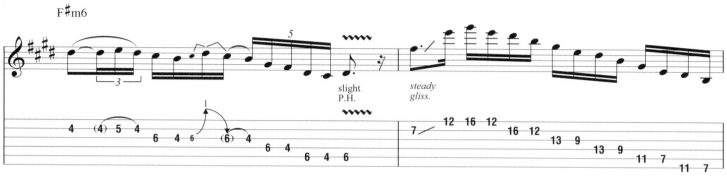

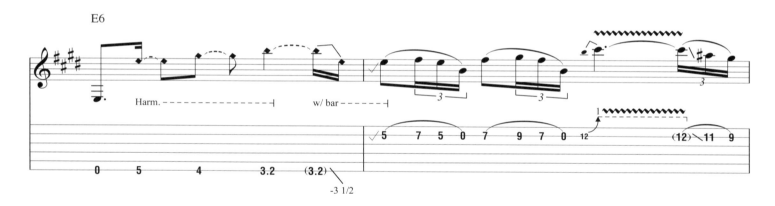

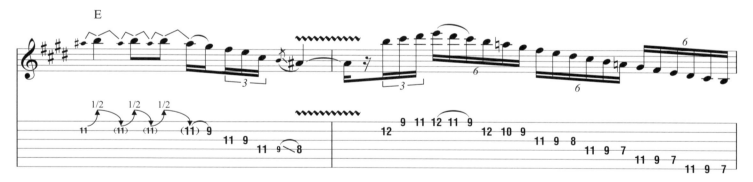

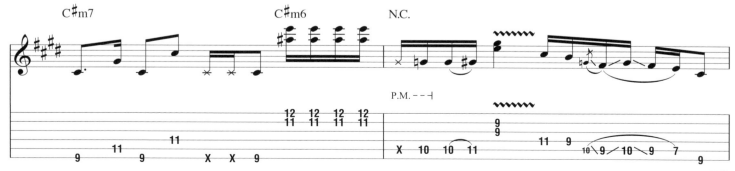

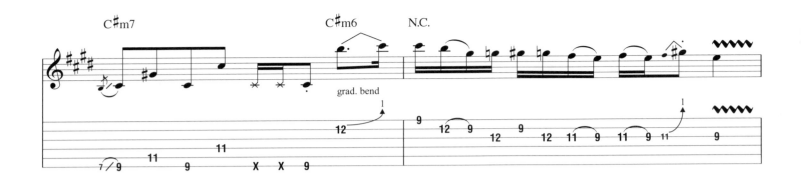

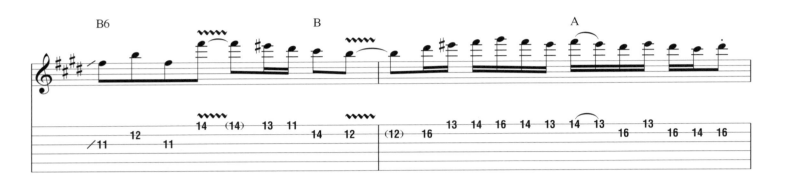

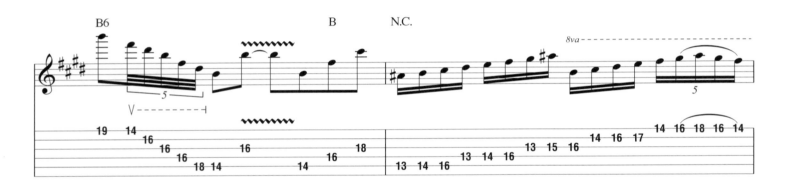

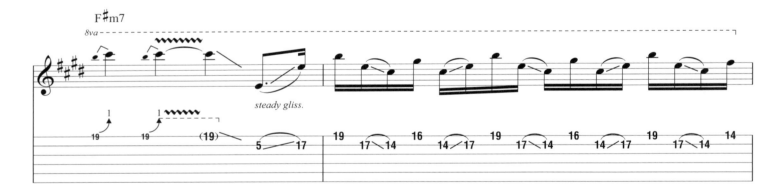

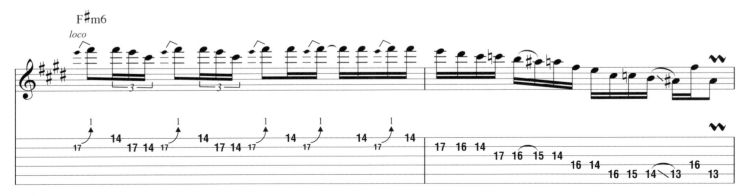

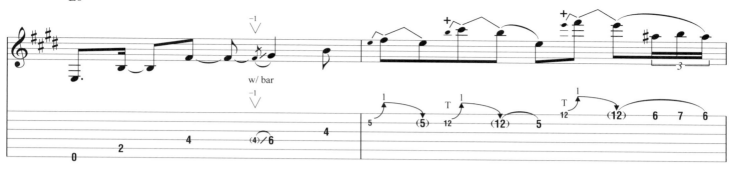

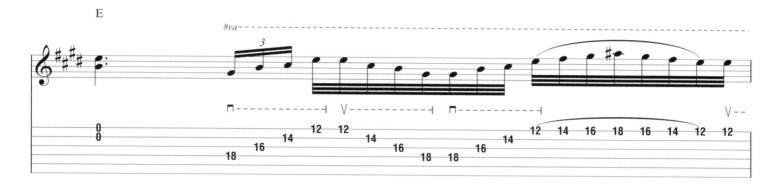

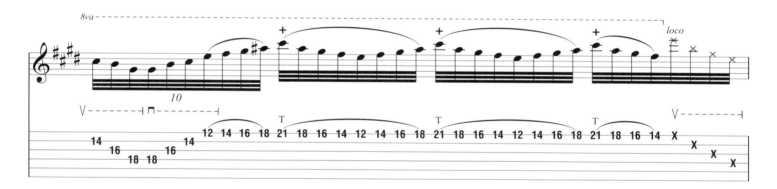

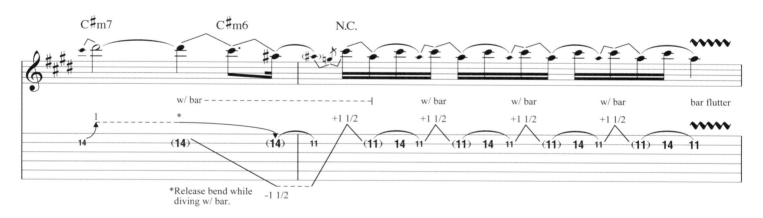

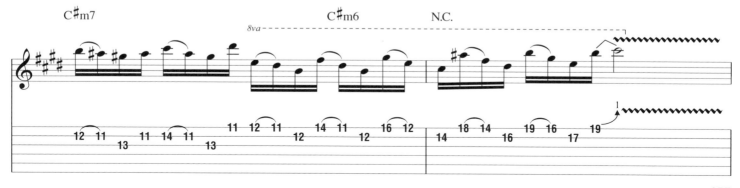

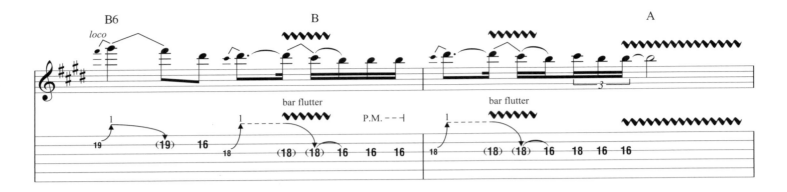

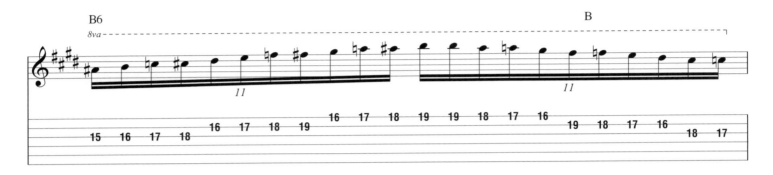

Keyboard Solo

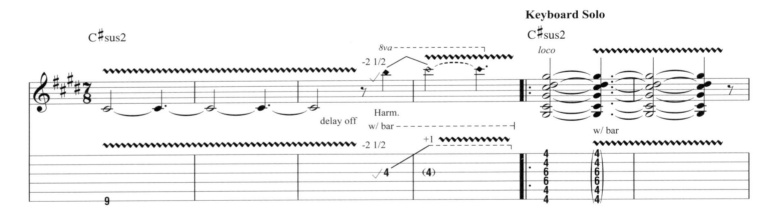

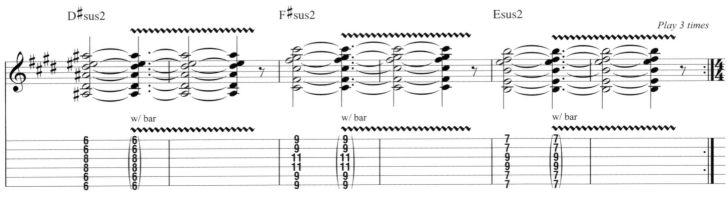

pray - ing _____ for time _____ to dis - ap - pear. _____

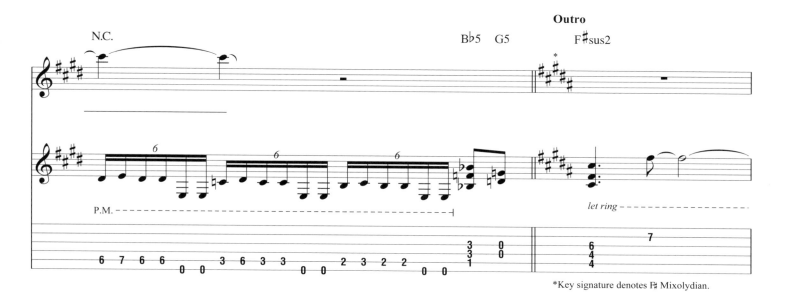

*Key signature denotes F♯ Mixolydian.

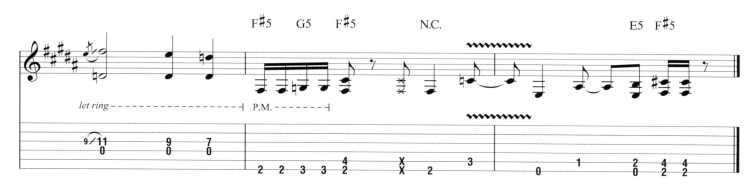

HAL•LEONARD GUITAR PLAY-ALONG

This series will help you play your favorite songs quickly and easily. Just follow the tab **INCLUDES TAB** and listen to the audio to the hear how the guitar should sound, and then play along using the separate backing tracks. Mac or PC users can also slow down the tempo without changing pitch by using the CD in their computer. The melody and lyrics are included in the book so that you can sing or simply follow along.

VOL. 1 – ROCK	00699570 / $16.99	
VOL. 2 – ACOUSTIC	00699569 / $16.95	
VOL. 3 – HARD ROCK	00699573 / $16.95	
VOL. 4 – POP/ROCK	00699571 / $16.99	
VOL. 5 – MODERN ROCK	00699574 / $16.99	
VOL. 6 – '90S ROCK	00699572 / $16.99	
VOL. 7 – BLUES	00699575 / $16.95	
VOL. 8 – ROCK	00699585 / $14.99	
VOL. 10 – ACOUSTIC	00699586 / $16.95	
VOL. 11 – EARLY ROCK	00699579 / $14.95	
VOL. 12 – POP/ROCK	00699587 / $14.95	
VOL. 13 – FOLK ROCK	00699581 / $15.99	
VOL. 14 – BLUES ROCK	00699582 / $16.95	
VOL. 15 – R&B	00699583 / $14.95	
VOL. 16 – JAZZ	00699584 / $15.95	
VOL. 17 – COUNTRY	00699588 / $15.95	
VOL. 18 – ACOUSTIC ROCK	00699577 / $15.95	
VOL. 19 – SOUL	00699578 / $14.99	
VOL. 20 – ROCKABILLY	00699580 / $14.95	
VOL. 21 – YULETIDE	00699602 / $14.95	
VOL. 22 – CHRISTMAS	00699600 / $15.95	
VOL. 23 – SURF	00699635 / $14.95	
VOL. 24 – ERIC CLAPTON	00699649 / $17.99	
VOL. 25 – LENNON & MCCARTNEY	00699642 / $16.99	
VOL. 26 – ELVIS PRESLEY	00699643 / $14.95	
VOL. 27 – DAVID LEE ROTH	00699645 / $16.95	
VOL. 28 – GREG KOCH	00699646 / $14.95	
VOL. 29 – BOB SEGER	00699647 / $15.99	
VOL. 30 – KISS	00699644 / $16.99	
VOL. 31 – CHRISTMAS HITS	00699652 / $14.95	
VOL. 32 – THE OFFSPRING	00699653 / $14.95	
VOL. 33 – ACOUSTIC CLASSICS	00699656 / $16.95	
VOL. 34 – CLASSIC ROCK	00699658 / $16.95	
VOL. 35 – HAIR METAL	00699660 / $16.95	
VOL. 36 – SOUTHERN ROCK	00699661 / $16.95	
VOL. 37 – ACOUSTIC UNPLUGGED	00699662 / $22.99	
VOL. 38 – BLUES	00699663 / $16.95	
VOL. 39 – '80S METAL	00699664 / $16.99	
VOL. 40 – INCUBUS	00699668 / $17.95	
VOL. 41 – ERIC CLAPTON	00699669 / $16.95	
VOL. 42 – 2000S ROCK	00699670 / $16.99	
VOL. 43 – LYNYRD SKYNYRD	00699681 / $17.95	
VOL. 44 – JAZZ	00699689 / $14.99	
VOL. 45 – TV THEMES	00699718 / $14.95	
VOL. 46 – MAINSTREAM ROCK	00699722 / $16.95	
VOL. 47 – HENDRIX SMASH HITS	00699723 / $19.95	
VOL. 48 – AEROSMITH CLASSICS	00699724 / $17.99	
VOL. 49 – STEVIE RAY VAUGHAN	00699725 / $17.99	
VOL. 50 – VAN HALEN 1978-1984	00110269 / $17.99	
VOL. 51 – ALTERNATIVE '90S	00699727 / $14.99	
VOL. 52 – FUNK	00699728 / $14.95	
VOL. 53 – DISCO	00699729 / $14.99	
VOL. 54 – HEAVY METAL	00699730 / $14.95	
VOL. 55 – POP METAL	00699731 / $14.95	
VOL. 56 – FOO FIGHTERS	00699749 / $15.99	
VOL. 57 – SYSTEM OF A DOWN	00699751 / $14.95	
VOL. 58 – BLINK-182	00699772 / $14.95	
VOL. 59 – CHET ATKINS	00702347 / $16.99	
VOL. 60 – 3 DOORS DOWN	00699774 / $14.95	
VOL. 61 – SLIPKNOT	00699775 / $16.99	
VOL. 62 – CHRISTMAS CAROLS	00699798 / $12.95	
VOL. 63 – CREEDENCE CLEARWATER REVIVAL	00699802 / $16.99	
VOL. 64 – THE ULTIMATE OZZY OSBOURNE	00699803 / $16.99	
VOL. 66 – THE ROLLING STONES	00699807 / $16.95	
VOL. 67 – BLACK SABBATH	00699808 / $16.99	
VOL. 68 – PINK FLOYD – DARK SIDE OF THE MOON	00699809 / $16.99	
VOL. 69 – ACOUSTIC FAVORITES	00699810 / $14.95	
VOL. 70 – OZZY OSBOURNE	00699805 / $16.99	
VOL. 71 – CHRISTIAN ROCK	00699824 / $14.95	
VOL. 73 – BLUESY ROCK	00699829 / $16.99	
VOL. 75 – TOM PETTY	00699882 / $16.99	
VOL. 76 – COUNTRY HITS	00699884 / $14.95	
VOL. 77 – BLUEGRASS	00699910 / $14.99	
VOL. 78 – NIRVANA	00700132 / $16.99	
VOL. 79 – NEIL YOUNG	00700133 / $24.99	
VOL. 80 – ACOUSTIC ANTHOLOGY	00700175 / $19.95	
VOL. 81 – ROCK ANTHOLOGY	00700176 / $22.99	
VOL. 82 – EASY SONGS	00700177 / $12.99	
VOL. 83 – THREE CHORD SONGS	00700178 / $16.99	
VOL. 84 – STEELY DAN	00700200 / $16.99	
VOL. 85 – THE POLICE	00700269 / $16.99	
VOL. 86 – BOSTON	00700465 / $16.99	
VOL. 87 – ACOUSTIC WOMEN	00700763 / $14.99	
VOL. 88 – GRUNGE	00700467 / $16.99	
VOL. 89 – REGGAE	00700468 / $15.99	
VOL. 90 – CLASSICAL POP	00700469 / $14.99	
VOL. 91 – BLUES INSTRUMENTALS	00700505 / $14.99	
VOL. 92 – EARLY ROCK INSTRUMENTALS	00700506 / $14.99	
VOL. 93 – ROCK INSTRUMENTALS	00700507 / $16.99	
VOL. 94 – SLOW BLUES	00700508 / $16.99	
VOL. 95 – BLUES CLASSICS	00700509 / $14.99	
VOL. 96 – THIRD DAY	00700560 / $14.95	
VOL. 97 – ROCK BAND	00700703 / $14.99	
VOL. 99 – ZZ TOP	00700762 / $16.99	
VOL. 100 – B.B. KING	00700466 / $16.99	
VOL. 101 – SONGS FOR BEGINNERS	00701917 / $14.99	
VOL. 102 – CLASSIC PUNK	00700769 / $14.99	
VOL. 103 – SWITCHFOOT	00700773 / $16.99	
VOL. 104 – DUANE ALLMAN	00700846 / $16.99	
VOL. 105 – LATIN	00700939 / $16.99	
VOL. 106 – WEEZER	00700958 / $14.99	
VOL. 107 – CREAM	00701069 / $16.99	
VOL. 108 – THE WHO	00701053 / $16.99	
VOL. 109 – STEVE MILLER	00701054 / $14.99	
VOL. 110 – SLIDE GUITAR HITS	00701055 / $16.99	
VOL. 111 – JOHN MELLENCAMP	00701056 / $14.99	
VOL. 112 – QUEEN	00701052 / $16.99	
VOL. 113 – JIM CROCE	00701058 / $15.99	
VOL. 114 – BON JOVI	00701060 / $14.99	
VOL. 115 – JOHNNY CASH	00701070 / $16.99	
VOL. 116 – THE VENTURES	00701124 / $14.99	
VOL. 117 – BRAD PAISLEY	00701224 / $16.99	
VOL. 118 – ERIC JOHNSON	00701353 / $16.99	
VOL. 119 – AC/DC CLASSICS	00701356 / $17.99	
VOL. 120 – PROGRESSIVE ROCK	00701457 / $14.99	
VOL. 121 – U2	00701508 / $16.99	
VOL. 122 – CROSBY, STILLS & NASH	00701610 / $16.99	
VOL. 123 – LENNON & MCCARTNEY ACOUSTIC	00701614 / $16.99	
VOL. 125 – JEFF BECK	00701687 / $16.99	
VOL. 126 – BOB MARLEY	00701701 / $16.99	
VOL. 127 – 1970S ROCK	00701739 / $14.99	
VOL. 128 – 1960S ROCK	00701740 / $14.99	
VOL. 129 – MEGADETH	00701741 / $16.99	
VOL. 131 – 1990S ROCK	00701743 / $14.99	
VOL. 132 – COUNTRY ROCK	00701757 / $15.99	
VOL. 133 – TAYLOR SWIFT	00701894 / $16.99	
VOL. 134 – AVENGED SEVENFOLD	00701906 / $16.99	
VOL. 136 – GUITAR THEMES	00701922 / $14.99	
VOL. 137 – IRISH TUNES	00701966 / $15.99	
VOL. 138 – BLUEGRASS CLASSICS	00701967 / $14.99	
VOL. 139 – GARY MOORE	00702370 / $16.99	
VOL. 140 – MORE STEVIE RAY VAUGHAN	00702396 / $17.99	
VOL. 141 – ACOUSTIC HITS	00702401 / $16.99	
VOL. 143 – SLASH	00702425 / $19.99	
VOL. 144 – DJANGO REINHARDT	00702531 / $16.99	
VOL. 145 – DEF LEPPARD	00702532 / $16.99	
VOL. 146 – ROBERT JOHNSON	00702533 / $16.99	
VOL. 147 – SIMON & GARFUNKEL	14041591 / $16.99	
VOL. 148 – BOB DYLAN	14041592 / $16.99	
VOL. 149 – AC/DC HITS	14041593 / $17.99	
VOL. 150 – ZAKK WYLDE	02501717 / $16.99	
VOL. 152 – JOE BONAMASSA	02501751 / $19.99	
VOL. 153 – RED HOT CHILI PEPPERS	00702990 / $19.99	
VOL. 155 – ERIC CLAPTON – FROM THE ALBUM UNPLUGGED	00703085 / $16.99	
VOL. 156 – SLAYER	00703770 / $17.99	
VOL. 157 – FLEETWOOD MAC	00101382 / $16.99	
VOL. 158 – ULTIMATE CHRISTMAS	00101889 / $14.99	
VOL. 159 – WES MONTGOMERY	00102593 / $19.99	
VOL. 160 – T-BONE WALKER	00102641 / $16.99	
VOL. 161 – THE EAGLES – ACOUSTIC	00102659 / $17.99	
VOL. 162 – THE EAGLES HITS	00102667 / $17.99	
VOL. 163 – PANTERA	00103036 / $17.99	
VOL. 164 – VAN HALEN 1986-1995	00110270 / $17.99	
VOL. 166 – MODERN BLUES	00700764 / $16.99	
VOL. 168 – KISS	00113421 / $16.99	
VOL. 169 – TAYLOR SWIFT	00115982 / $16.99	
VOL. 170 – THREE DAYS GRACE	00117337 / $16.99	
VOL. 171 – JAMES BROWN	00117420 / $16.99	
VOL. 172 – THE DOOBIE BROTHERS	00119670 / $16.99	
VOL. 174 – SCORPIONS	00122119 / $16.99	
VOL. 175 – MICHAEL SCHENKER	00122127 / $16.99	
VOL. 176 – BLUES BREAKERS WITH JOHN MAYALL & ERIC CLAPTON	00122132 / $19.99	
VOL. 177 – ALBERT KING	00123271 / $16.99	
VOL. 178 – JASON MRAZ	00124165 / $17.99	
VOL. 179 – RAMONES	00127073 / $16.99	
VOL. 180 – BRUNO MARS	00129706 / $16.99	
VOL. 181 – JACK JOHNSON	00129854 / $16.99	
VOL. 182 – SOUNDGARDEN	00138161 / $17.99	
VOL. 184 – KENNY WAYNE SHEPHERD	00138258 / $17.99	
VOL. 187 – JOHN DENVER	00140839 / $17.99	

Complete song lists available online.

Prices, contents, and availability subject to change without notice.

HAL•LEONARD® CORPORATION
7777 W. BLUEMOUND RD. P.O. BOX 13819 MILWAUKEE, WI 53213
www.halleonard.com

1215